Just Between God & Me

To Debbie   1978

from Manfords

Just Between God & Me

Sandra Drescher

ZONDERVAN
PUBLISHING HOUSE

OF THE ZONDERVAN CORPORATION | GRAND RAPIDS, MICHIGAN 49506

Scripture quotations are taken from the following:

The New International Version — New Testament (NIV). Copyright © 1973 by New York International Bible Society.

The Living Bible (LB). Copyright © 1971 by Tyndale House Publishers, Wheaton, Illinois. Used by permission.

The Revised Standard Version (RSV). Copyright © 1946, 1952 by the Division of Christian Education of the National Council of Churches of Christ in the United States of America.

JUST BETWEEN GOD AND ME

© 1977 by The Zondervan Corporation
Grand Rapids, Michigan

Library of Congress Cataloging in Publication Data
Drescher, Sandra.
    Just between God and me.
    SUMMARY: Includes a meditation, Scripture verse, and
short prayer for every day of the year.
    1.   Youth—Prayer-books and devotions—English.
[1.   Prayer books and devotions]   I.   Title.
BV4850.D73   242'.6'3   76-51295

Fifth printing   October 1977

Cloth: Girls: ISBN 0-310-23940-0
Cloth: Boys: ISBN 0-310-23950-8
Paper: ISBN 0-310-23941-9

Printed in the United States of America

To DAD,
who has given me love, guidance, and
encouragement in writing and growing,
and
to MOTHER,
who is one of my closest friends
in the adventure of discovering life.

A NEW DAY

Father, I know that all my life
Is portioned out for me;
The changes that are sure to come
I do not fear to see;
I ask Thee for a present mind
Intent on pleasing Thee.

On this first day of the year these words by Henry Drummond have a special meaning for me. It's great to begin a year with the knowledge that the God who made me has a plan for me and that I need not fear the future. As a young person, sometimes I have a fear of the future. But I find that when I'm intent on pleasing God, my fear fades away and God gives me faith for the day.

Fear not, for I am with you. Do not be dismayed. I am your God. I will strengthen you; I will help you; I will uphold you with my victorious right hand (Isa. 41:10 LB).

Lord, since yesterday cannot be recalled and tomorrow cannot be assured, help me make the most of today. Teach me this coming year how to use each day for Your glory and to do Your will. Amen.

STARTING OVER

At the beginning of the new year, the past is forgotten and new resolutions are made. But it is easy to get carried away with all the festivities and forget our greatest and most important Friend — Jesus.

I know I need Jesus to begin the new year. What I sometimes forget is that I need to go through each day with Him.

I must have His help in carrying out my good intentions day by day. Even when the days tend to become monotonous, Jesus can bring new life and meaning.

And may your strength match the length of your days! (Deut. 33:25 LB).

Jesus, be with me throughout this new year as I learn to trust in You more and more. Make each day meaningful, and teach me to receive the strength You give daily. Amen.

MY LIFE — GOD'S STORY

My life is like a story, with God as its Author. I live my story at the same speed as everyone else, and only the Author knows what will happen next. That makes it exciting!

Some chapters are sad and discouraging, but these make the good chapters seem even better. All moods are necessary to create a good story. Otherwise it might become dull.

The clue to getting the most enjoyment out of my story is to figure out what God is trying to communicate to me through each page and then to act upon it. I've found that I'm happiest dwelling on the good chapters rather than on the bitter, lonely ones; and I must remember to give God the glory when others read part of my story and like it. After all, the Author should receive the credit for what He has written.

You saw me before I was born and scheduled each day of my life before I began to breathe. Every day was recorded in your Book! (Ps. 139:16 LB).

God, You have made a good story for my life so far, and I trust

You to continue writing it. Thank You for being in charge. Amen.

THREADS OF LIFE

A poem I found describes in a slightly different way the feeling I expressed in yesterday's meditation.

> Not until each loom is silent
> And the shuttles cease to fly,
> Will God unroll the pattern
> And explain the reason why
> The dark threads are so needful
> In the Weaver's skillful hand
> As the threads of gold and silver
> For the pattern which He planned.
> — Anonymous

Even though I don't understand why some moments in life are dark and miserable, God has a purpose for them, just as He does for the good times.

But when I am afraid, I will put my confidence in you. Yes, I will trust the promises of God (Ps. 56:3 LB).

Thank You, Jesus, for taking care of my life so I don't need to worry about anything. I only need to trust You. Amen.

THY WILL BE DONE

My father keeps a short prayer in his date book. He told me he has carried it with him since his high school days when a friend first shared it with him.

Renew my will from day to day,
Blend it with Thine
And take away
All that now makes it hard to say
Thy will be done.

Although the author is unknown, the prayer captures beautifully the deep desire of a committed Christian. It also conveys the prayer I want to keep in my heart this new year.

Help me do your will, for you are my God (Ps. 143:10 LB).

Lord, each day may I sincerely say, "I delight in doing Your will." I know Your will is best, and yet I find it easy to want my own will. Forgive me, and teach me to do Your will. Amen.

January 6

THE SOLE MEDIATOR

While reading Dietrich Bonhoeffer's book *The Cost of Discipleship*, I came into a new awareness of my life through Christ. Jesus is the Mediator between God and man. He is also the Mediator between man and man, and between man and reality. Because He is the only God, He is therefore the only Mediator, and He comes between everything. Since I was made by Christ, He is the Mediator between me and anything or anyone I communicate with. It's good to know that God is with me all the time, in every conversation and situation.

Yet for us there is but one God, the Father, from whom all things came and for whom we live; and there is but one Lord, Jesus Christ, through whom all things came and through whom we live (1 Cor. 8:6 NIV).

Thank You, Lord, for being the Mediator so I can communicate to all that is around me. Amen.

GOOD MORNING, LORD!

Getting up each morning at the same time, going to school, rushing through classes and meals, doing homework, and going to bed, only to get up the following day to the same routine, can become monotonous and meaningless. Is this the kind of life Christ has planned for His followers?

A day started by a quiet time with the Lord makes a lot of difference in my life. The rest of my day becomes a new adventure with Jesus by my side. His continual presence helps the events fall in place in a unique way. When I say, "Good morning, Lord! What do You have for us to do together today?" it makes every moment vibrant with expectancy and excitement. I am aware that He's directing each step.

In everything you do, put God first, and he will direct you and crown your efforts with success (Prov. 3:6 LB).

Good morning, Lord! Thank You for being with me continually in everything I do. Let's go through this day together. Amen.

REAL WORTH

Many advertisements try to sell products which attempt to persuade me to become a better person by looking, feeling, or smelling a certain way. I often get discouraged by seeing such nonsense wherever I go. Advertisers seem to have missed the whole point of a person's worth. They insist that proper looks are more important than a proper heart and actions, as Jesus teaches.

Jesus is far more interested in what kind of a person I am on the inside, than merely what I appear to be on the outside.

> **Shout that man is like the grass that dies away, and all his beauty fades like dying flowers. . . . The grass withers, the flowers fade, but the Word of our God shall stand forever (Isa. 40:6,8 LB).**

Lord, keep ever present in my mind the knowledge that outside beauty is only temporary. Inside beauty is what counts for eternity. Amen.

January 9

WALK ABOVE THE WAVES

This morning I read the story in Matthew 14 of Peter's walk on the water. The water was calm as Peter began his journey toward Jesus. But when he thought about the potential danger, he became frightened and started to sink, crying out for the Lord's help. Immediately Jesus was there to rescue him.

That's how it is in my Christian life. When I keep my eyes fixed on Jesus, it's possible to walk through storms and stay on top of my problems, knowing that, with Jesus by my side, they won't get the best of me. But as soon as I take my eyes off Jesus, and instead see only the dangerous winds and waves of life's trials, I begin to sink.

What's great is that each time I call for Jesus to rescue me, He's right there, waiting patiently to lift me up again.

> **Immediately Jesus reached out his hand and caught him. "You of little faith," he said, "why did you doubt?" (Matt. 14:31 NIV).**

Thank You, Jesus, for always staying near to help me rise above the waves and not sink in every little storm. Amen.

RICH OR POOR?

When I was small, I thought our family was poor. We didn't have a swimming pool or tennis courts like some of my friends did nor did I have as many clothes as they.

Since then I've discovered that in a different and more important way, I am many times richer than those who are rich in material possessions. Whether I'm rich or not depends on how I view life and with whom I'm comparing myself.

I didn't bring anything into this life, and I can't take anything with me. No matter how long these years seem, time on earth is extremely short compared to eternity. This is home to me, but really I'm only a stranger living here for awhile. My real home is in heaven. Therefore, true richness consists only of what is eternally important.

My riches are found in fellowship with good Christian friends and with God, a loving family, the privilege of living where I'm free to worship God as I choose, a mind to think and reason, creativity to keep life exciting, and many other things. The world might not classify these as riches, but they are really the greatest riches anyone can attain.

What profit is there if you gain the whole world — and lose eternal life? What can be compared with the value of eternal life? (Matt. 16:26 LB).

Heavenly Father, keep me always striving for life's true riches and not getting sidetracked into thinking the things of this world are most important. Only You can provide true riches. Amen.

GOD STILL SPEAKS

Often I tend to believe God spoke to people in the Bible more directly than He speaks to me today. It's a good excuse for not doing something. I think, "God didn't say it out loud from the sky, so how do I know for sure?"

Last year our class had an assignment to put ourselves in Abraham's place and write a first-person account of how he felt when God told him to sacrifice his only son, Isaac, as a burnt offering. The stories were interesting, but one in particular brought out a new thought. I had been under the impression that God spoke to Abraham in an audible voice, but one person wrote that maybe God just put the thought in Abraham's mind. Abraham had enough faith in God to do what He told him, even though it may not have been in as concrete terms as speaking aloud.

That made me wonder how concretely I'd have to hear God's voice to obey. I hope I won't evade conviction just because God doesn't speak audibly to me.

I waited patiently for God to help me; then he listened and heard my cry (Ps. 40:1 LB).

Let me know Your wishes, God, in whatever way You think is best. Help me to know Your will and follow it. Amen.

January 12

FINDING HIS WILL

Some time ago, a friend and I were discussing how God speaks to us today. Neither of us had ever been spoken to by a voice from heaven. We knew God has ways of speaking directly to His people, but sometimes it's hard to determine what He is saying to us.

The next day we were traveling on an interstate highway. We didn't need gas right away, but we decided to stop anyway. After the service station attendant filled the gas tank, he noticed smoke coming out from under the hood. He checked it, and the hole he found could have meant disaster if we had driven any farther. If we had stopped for gas sooner, it wouldn't have been noticeable yet.

We felt God had His hand in that situation and was showing us one of the ways He talks to us today. I must always try to be aware of what God's trying to tell me in whatever way He chooses.

Many blessings are given to those who trust the Lord (Ps. 40:4 LB).

Thank You, Lord, for speaking to me today. Help me to know when it's You talking, or if my desires are getting mixed up in Yours. Amen.

January 13

I'M RESPONSIBLE FOR ME

When I'm trying to decide what to do, a big consideration I take into account is what my friends are doing. That's not always bad, but it can be. It's easy to forget my own values and think something can't be wrong if so many of my friends are doing it.

While friends, especially Christian friends, can be of help, it is most important to remember that when God looks at my life, He doesn't consider how many others did the same things I did. He holds me, alone, responsible for my actions, words, and thoughts. I must keep what I do in perspective with what Christ wants of me, without blindly following others.

So then, each of us will give an account of himself to God (Rom. 14:12 NIV).

I am looking to You, Lord, for guidance in my daily walk with You. Amen.

MAGNIFY THE LORD

Binoculars are fun to use. With them, distant objects become much larger and clearer, as though I am closer.

The Bible talks of magnifying the name of the Lord. When I compare this with how things are magnified through binoculars, its meaning becomes more real.

God can't really be enlarged or made stronger, but I can make Him seem closer in my mind. When I cut out the background, foreground, and sideviews, which distract me from focusing my attention on Him alone, I can see His ways more clearly and be drawn closer to Him. Jesus remains the same, waiting for me to magnify Him.

Christ shall be magnified in my body, whether it be by life, or by death (Phil. 1:20 KJV).

Jesus, I want to learn better how to magnify You. Teach me to focus on You alone. Amen.

A HELP IN TROUBLE

A woman came to church with an exciting story to share. She had been watching an ant carry a piece of straw. The straw was small, but it seemed large to the ant. The ant came to a channel of water, also tiny, but dangerous to the ant. Instead of giving up and quitting, the ant put the straw across the water, crawled on it, picked up the straw, and went on.

The story reminded me of how my life must look in God's eyes. I face many situations which look dangerous and threatening to me, but God sees how easily I could overcome the problem, so He gives me help and strength. He doesn't allow me to face any situation that is impossible for me to handle, but He helps me find a way over the rough spots.

Take a lesson from the ants, you lazy fellow. Learn from their ways and be wise! (Prov. 6:6 LB).

Thank You, Lord, for caring so much about me and helping me through all life's trials. Amen.

LETTING GOD USE ME

A few years ago, a building near us was condemned because termites had eaten so much wood that it wasn't safe any more. Later it was torn down because nothing could be done with it. The termites had completely destroyed it.

To think that something as small as a termite could do so much damage! When I think about the vastness of our world and universe, I feel small and insignificant; but the termites taught me a good lesson. Everything I do has some impact, and it's up to me to determine whether it's good or bad. If little termites can ruin a big building, I can do something far greater for good, if I'm willing to work at it.

God can use the smallest deeds of goodness for His glory. Even if no one else sees it, God will reward fully.

May the Lord God of Israel, under whose wings you have come to take refuge, bless you for it (Ruth 2:12 LB).

Father, help me to think about what good I can do, instead of feeling small and insignificant. Amen.

WHAT A FRIEND!

The blind poet George Matheson wrote:

> There is an Eye that never sleeps
> Beneath the wing of night;
> There is an Ear that never shuts
> When sink the beams of light;
> There is an Arm that never tires
> When human strength gives way;
> There is a Love that never fails
> When earthly loves decay.

It's almost too unbelievable to know that I have such a friend!

How precious it is, Lord, to realize that you are thinking about me constantly! I can't even count how many times a day your thoughts turn towards me (Ps. 139:17 LB).

God, Your constant love overwhelms me! How can I begin to praise You enough? Amen.

FRUIT OF THE SPIRIT

Recently I made a surprising discovery. In reading about the fruit of the Holy Spirit, I noticed that *fruit* is always written in the singular. Putting it that way indicates that each Christian has some of each fruit and not just some of one or two.

Unlike the gifts of the Spirit — one Christian usually doesn't have all of the gifts — I am responsible, by the Holy Spirit's power, to nurture each fruit and allow it to grow.

Bearing fruit is a quiet, steady process, flourishing best in situations where I relate to others who are also growing Spirit fruit. By producing the fruit of the Spirit in greater abundance, the Holy Spirit's presence in my life becomes more evident.

> **But when the Holy Spirit controls our lives he will produce this kind of fruit in us: love, joy, peace, patience, kindness, goodness, faithfulness, gentleness and self-control; and here there is no conflict with Jewish laws (Gal. 5:22 LB).**

I pray that Your Spirit will work freely in my life to strengthen the fruit of love, joy, peace, patience, kindness, goodness, faithfulness, gentleness, and self-control. Amen.

January 19

MORE FRUIT

Like the producer of any fruit, a Christian growing Spirit fruit needs to be pruned in order to produce at his best.

When I sincerely ask for more of any one fruit, I can expect trying situations to help that fruit to mature. I recall a time when I prayed for patience to become more real in me. In the weeks that followed, God put many situations in my life that tested my patience. They weren't easy, but I know it was a loving answer to my prayer.

Pruning can be painful, but it is necessary for the best and fullest production. Christ prunes me as I need it and as I'm ready.

> **Since we live by the Spirit, let us keep in step with the Spirit (Gal. 5:25 NIV).**

Thank You, Lord, for helping me grow in the fruit of Your Spirit. Don't spare me the pain of pruning, but teach me Your ways. Amen.

THE SIMPLE LIFE STYLE

José Ortiz is a brilliant young Puerto Rican Christian leader who has come to the United States to lead the Spanish churches. Recently at a conference I heard him speak about the Christian life style of simple living. He described the Christian life style as simply "caring more about persons than things."

A person may live in a hut with few of life's possessions, yet be a miser and unconcerned about others. Poverty, or the denial of things, in itself, is hardly Christian.

Putting people ahead of things determines how I use my time, my money, and my possessions, which in turn produces a certain life style. As a Christian who wants to live a simple life style, I should be considering what I can do for others instead of wondering what I might have to give up.

Blessed are the poor in spirit, for theirs is the kingdom of heaven (Matt. 5:3 NIV).

Lord, grant that I may seek to serve people, not things. Instill in me a care for others. Amen.

WHY WORRY?

In all the activity of school, home, and church life, I tend to worry a lot about how I'll get everything done and whether everything will work out right. I am tempted to worry about a lot of things. It may seem to an observer that I translate the verse that says, "Don't worry about tomorrow, for your heavenly Father will take care of you" into "Worry your head off about tomorrow for if you don't, things won't turn out right."

Too often I forget that God has promised to take care of all my problems, and He's the only one who has the power to change a situation for me anyway. It's actually an insult to God for me to worry, because I'm saying, "God, I don't think You can handle this situation, so I'm going to worry about it."

Let him have all your worries and cares, for he is always thinking about you and watching everything that concerns you (1 Peter 5:7 LB).

Thank You, Lord, for being my constant protector. You know what is best for me. Keep me trusting in You instead of worrying. Amen.

January 22

WASTED WORRY

Not only is worry needless for a Christian, as we thought about yesterday, but it's also a waste of time. Someone wrote of worry:

40% will never happen, for anxiety is the result of a tired mind,
30% concerns old decisions which cannot be altered,
12% centers in criticisms, mostly untrue, made by people who feel inferior,
10% is related to my health which worsens while I worry, and only
8% is "legitimate," showing that life does have real problems which may be met head on when I have eliminated senseless worries.

Many of us spend half our time wishing for things we could have if we didn't spend half our time wishing. As Philipp Melanchthon once said, "Trouble and perplexity drive us to prayer, and prayer drives away trouble and perplexity."

Don't worry about anything; instead, pray about everything; tell God your needs and don't forget to thank him for his answers (Phil. 4:6 LB).

With You, Father, I can see what a waste of time it is for me to worry. Help me to stay away from the sin of wasted worry. Amen.

TURN WORRY INTO FAITH

Worry can have a positive perspective. It can prove that I really am interested in a friend or a person God has given to me, or that I really care about a situation. Knowing what to do with that worry is what's important.

If I turn my worry into faith, my faith can be as strong as my worry was. One prayer does more good than many times that amount of time spent worrying. I need to pray for the faith necessary to control or overcome worry. To make the most of my worry, I have to turn it into faith in God to work everything out.

His peace will keep your thoughts and your hearts quiet and at rest as you trust in Christ Jesus (Phil. 4:7 LB).

Give me the ability, Jesus, to turn all my useless worry into a strong, powerful faith, that I may be closer to You. Amen.

WHAT IS FAITH?

Leslie D. Weatherhead, in his book *The Transforming Friendship*, tells an interesting story.

An old Scotsman found it impossible to pray. When he

tried, his thoughts wandered or he fell asleep. He became so worried that he spoke to his minister about it. The minister advised him to put a chair beside him, imagine Jesus sitting in the chair, and talk to Him as he would to a friend. By doing this, the Scotsman accepted the gift of friendship and made his Master real, not by intellect or will, but by an imagination which became faith. When he died, his arm was resting on the empty chair beside him.

Faith is believing Jesus is with me all the time and accepting His friendship as a gift. As the spelling of *faith* may suggest: Forsaking *A*ll, *I* Take *H*im. I have faith when I am willing to stake my life on Jesus.

The righteous will live by faith (Rom. 1:17 NIV).

O Master and Friend, guide me in Your ways. Be real to me so my faith will grow in You. Thank You. Amen.

HIS GIFT OF SALVATION

Giving gifts is fun. I love to see the joy others receive when given a gift and the joy of the giver for being able to cheer up someone else's day.

I've also seen the hurt which comes when a gift is rejected. When someone can't accept even the smallest gift of kindness, joy is taken out of the giving. Jesus has a greater gift to give to each one of His children than we can comprehend — His gift of salvation. By accepting this gift, life is made more joyful for everyone involved.

Thanks be to God for his indescribable gift! (2 Cor. 9:15 NIV).

Thank You, Savior, for giving me the gift of salvation. Amen.

WALKING WITH JESUS

As a child, each day before I ran to the bus stop for school, I prayed this short prayer with mother:

> Starting out this morning, this is what I pray,
> Take my hand, dear Jesus, walk with me today.
> Then I'll just go places where you wish me to.
> I'll be safe and happy, hand in hand with you.

The prayer remained with me as I grew older, but it has added meaning. Now I have a clearer understanding of what it means to walk each day, hand in hand with Jesus. It feels good to have someone to keep me safe and happy, someone who will never leave me. It feels good to have the knowledge of His constant guidance.

I am holding you by your right hand — I, the Lord your God — and I say to you, Don't be afraid; I am here to help you (Isa. 41:13 LB).

Take my hand, dear Jesus, walk with me today. And I'll be safe and happy, hand in hand with You. Amen.

LIVING MOMENT BY MOMENT

When the fourth person from my high school class was suddenly killed in a car accident, I, along with others, began to take a new look at life. Death was no longer something that happened to someone else in the distant future.

I began to examine my priorities in life and question whether or not they were really important. Questions like this became very real: If I had one day left on earth, would I be living the same way and doing the same things I am now? Could any relationships be improved? Do my friends and family know how much I appreciate them? And most important — Does God know I love Him?

Our lives are so unpredictable. We can't look ahead and think we'll take care of something tomorrow or next week. Living one moment at a time and doing what is eternally significant right now is most important.

> **Lord, help me to realize how brief my time on earth will be. Help me to know that I am here for but a moment more (Ps. 39:4 LB).**

God, I love You. I want to live for You, which means doing what You want me to do every moment of my life. Guide me in making the right decisions. Amen.

January 28

MY FACE — A MIRROR

It's fun to watch people. By looking at their faces, I can usually tell how they're feeling inside. Faces are like mirrors, reflecting what's going on underneath.

It's easy to forget how much my face tells about me and think no one else will notice. It's not too hard to look happy when I *am* happy; but when I'm *not* happy — that's when the real test comes. Sometimes it's hard to smile, but it's not fair to make others miserable just because I'm feeling a little down. As Myron Augsburger once said, "A forced smile is better than a sincere grouch."

> **And we, who with unveiled faces all reflect the Lord's glory, are being transformed into his likeness with ever-increasing glory, which comes from the Lord, who is the Spirit (2 Cor. 3:18 NIV).**

Master, may I learn to let Your joy radiate from my face, even when I may not be feeling my best. Amen.

PEACE

Saint Francis of Assisi penned a powerful prayer on peace which is a great challenge to me:
Lord,
    make me an instrument of Your peace.
    Where there is hatred let me sow love;
    Where there is injury, pardon;
    Where there is despair, hope;
    Where there is darkness, light; and
    Where there is sadness, joy.

O divine Master,
    grant that I may not so much
    Seek to be consoled as to console;
    To be understood as to understand;
    To be loved as to love;
    For it is in giving that we receive;
    It is in pardoning that we are pardoned; and
    It is in dying that we are born to eternal life.

. . . and in the shadow of death, to guide our feet into the path of peace (Luke 1:79 NIV).

Lord, may the prayer of Saint Francis be mine. Amen.

MEMORY — GOOD AND BAD

A good memory is useful when cramming for a test, learning lines for a play, memorizing Scripture, or listening to a lecture without needing to take notes.

However, a good memory can be a problem if too many of the wrong things are remembered. That single cutting remark, made in one short moment, may be remembered for months. A careless comment, made by a best friend, can ruin a relationship if it's dwelt on rather than being quickly forgiven and forgotten. Too many memories of a guy or girl you've dated in the past can result in a fantasy world instead of facing the reality that it's over. Memories will live on, but you can't live on memories.

Memories are good if they don't become a way of life. Right now life is too exciting to keep looking back.

Memories that remind me of the evil another person has done are never good. I need to get rid of them.

I am bringing all my energies to bear on this one thing: Forgetting the past and looking forward to what lies ahead (Phil. 3:13 LB).

Enable me, O Lord, to blot from my memory past remarks or events which serve only to nourish bitterness. Help me to press onward each day anew, and not be continually reminded of the past. Amen.

January 31

STAY NOURISHED

Our garden was growing well last summer. Everything was green, and the vegetables were developing beautifully. Then we had a drought and the plants began to wilt. They didn't receive the nourishment they needed to survive. Their roots hadn't grown deep enough to remain healthy.

I thought about that in relation to my life, finding the two to be much alike. As long as I have the proper nourishment from Christ, I continue to grow as a Christian, developing deeper, stronger roots in Him. But if that source is cut off, I quickly lose health and strength in my Christian life. The best way to be assured of continual growth is to spend time each day getting spiritual nourishment by reading what Jesus has to say through His Word and by talking with Him.

> Let your roots grow down into him and draw up nourishment from him. See that you go on growing in the Lord, and become strong and vigorous in the truth you were taught (Col. 2:7 LB).

Thank You, O Christ, for providing the nourishment I need to become strong spiritually. Help me to grow deep roots in living continually with You. Amen.

BRANCHES AND VINES

As I thought about spiritual nourishment, the analogy of Jesus as the Vine and His followers as the branches came to my mind.

A branch cannot live and grow unless it is attached to and is receiving nourishment from the vine. Only in keeping that contact can the branch hope to bear fruit.

My life works the same way. I can't survive on my own strength. I need Jesus Christ, as the Vine, to be attached to and to help me grow. After being supplied by Him for all my needs, I can produce a large crop of fruit which would be impossible if I tried to do it on my own.

If I would be separate from Jesus, my spiritual life would wither and be useless.

Yes, I am the Vine; you are the branches. Whoever lives in me and I in him shall produce a large crop of fruit. For apart from me you can't do a thing. If anyone separates from me, he is thrown away like a useless branch, withers, and is gathered into a pile with all the others and burned (John 15:5,6 LB).

You are the Vine, Jesus, and I want to be Your branch, depending on You for everything. Keep me hooked onto You so I don't wither and die. Amen.

PRUNING

Every year after our grapes, cherries, and roses are done bearing, my dad and brothers prune them. They cut them down so far it's hard to believe they will ever grow again, but actually it helps them produce more.

Jesus does the same thing in my life. Sometimes I feel like

He's done such a thorough job of pruning me that I'll never be able to grow back. But I have to remember that He's doing it out of love — to help me have more strength and usefulness for His kingdom. Pruning away the rotten or useless branches is a necessary part of growth if I want to produce more and better fruit. And being the perfect Gardener that He is, God never prunes me more than I can handle.

He cuts off every branch in me that bears no fruit, while every branch that does bear fruit he trims clean so that it will be even more fruitful (John 15:1 NIV).

Father, prune away the fruitless part of me as much as You think is right, and give me the strength to produce more fruit for You. Amen.

LIFE SCULPTURE

Michelangelo was asked how he did such a good job on his sculpture of David, to make it look so real. He replied that he had just chiseled away everything that wasn't David.

Christ can be that kind of sculptor in my life. He will chisel away all that isn't Christlike as long as I let Him.

Some of the chops and polishings may be hard to take or see the need for, but they're necessary in order to have the sculpture of my life look as Christlike as possible.

Do not conform any longer to the pattern of this world, but be transformed by the renewing of your mind (Rom. 12:1 NIV).

I pray, Lord, that I will keep turning my life over to You, so You can turn this sculpture into something that everyone will know is patterned after You. Amen.

MY CONSTANT FRIEND

When I was younger I had a best friend who lived nearby. We talked, played, and went everywhere together. Then she moved away. We wrote and visited each other, but it wasn't enough to keep our friendship close. When we were together after that, we were both aware that our relationship wasn't the same as before.

My relationship with God works the same way. When I spend time talking with Him and becoming more sensitive to His leading, our relationship is close. If I slack off, our relationship slacks off too. But I am thankful that He always waits for me and welcomes me back into His fellowship.

My God is changeless in his love for me and he will come and help me (Ps. 59:10 LB).

Thank You, Lord, that You're a constant friend, even when I'm unfaithful. I pray that I will always remain in Your love and care. Amen.

START EXPLORING

While reading part of an article written by Atlee Beachey, a college professor and counselor, I was struck by these words: "Your young years are years to explore, a time to discuss doubts and to examine your beliefs. Your temptation may be, however, to delay, to put off making a basic commitment. You may rationalize your delay by saying you are searching. You may delay moving into life until suddenly you discover that life is passing you by. You may throw off traditions and beliefs before affirming a new faith."

It's not always easy for me to think about what I believe and decide on my own set of values. Sometimes I'd rather just be a child a while longer and not think seriously about life. But that kind of an attitude can set a life pattern of not seriously considering the important decisions. To make life more meaningful now and for the future, the present is the best time to think about my beliefs, doubts, fears, and values, and to explore the true meaning of life.

Don't let the excitement of being young cause you to forget about your Creator (Eccl. 12:1 LB).

Lord, I'm ready to take You seriously and to let You be a real part of my life now and as I grow up. Live in me and help me make the necessary decisions. Amen.

February 6

BEING A FAITHFUL SERVANT

Sometimes the jobs assigned to me are so small and insignificant that they hardly seem worth doing. But as I do the minor jobs faithfully, I find that the responsibilities given to me become broader and more challenging. The first experiences were necessary in order to do a good job at bigger tasks.

God works the same way in my life. He doesn't look at how big and important my job is, but at how well I carry out whatever responsibility I have been given, no matter how unimportant.

For the man who uses well what he is given shall be given more, and he shall have abundance. But from the man who is unfaithful, even what little responsibility he has shall be taken from him (Matt. 25:29 LB).

May I always do the best with what I have, Jesus, to prepare me for even greater responsibilities. Amen.

HELP ME, LORD

Help me, Lord! I can't win this race alone. I'm too tired. Help me to remember all I learned and pass my exam today. Help me to learn all my lines for this play. Help me keep my patience through all this confusion.

These kinds of emergency prayers filled my days constantly. I thought God was glad I included Him in my problems, and He probably was; but then a new thought struck me. Where was God when I passed the exams or when I did win the race? I tended to shove Him back in a corner when I was joyful and only brought Him out when I needed help.

I soon found that praising God brings me closer to Him than simply praying "Help me" prayers. He deserves my praise and thanksgiving.

Think about all you can praise God for and be glad about (Phil. 4:8 LB).

Glorious Father, thank You for being near and waiting patiently for me to grow up. Thank You for being my closest Friend and giving me many good things in life. Amen.

BE AN INDIVIDUAL

A girl once wrote to a glamour columnist saying that she felt below the girls around her because she dressed differently. The columnist's advice to the girl was that she be herself and not try to copy everyone else — because each person has her own individuality.

God has given each person something special that no one

else has. This special individuality should not be suppressed but put to work for everyone's advantage. Only by developing my own unique personality will I ever be able to rise above average. God intended me to be an original, not a carbon copy of someone else.

He is loving and kind and rewards each one of us according to the work we do for him (Ps. 62:12 LB).

Lord, thank You for making me different from everyone else. Grant that I will always put my individuality to its best use for Your work. Amen.

February 9

LUCKY OR BLESSED?

"You're lucky!"
"I'm so lucky to be able to do this!"
These kinds of exclamations are often heard in everyday conversation. I didn't give much thought to the words until one day when I received a letter from a friend, who said, "It sometimes seems like I'm lucky . . . but I think God would be insulted if I thought that, because He planned it that way!"

That was a new and beautiful thought to me. Since God has my whole life planned, nothing that happens to me is chance or luck. It's God, carrying out His plan in me. When He wants to give me a blessing and I pass it off casually as good luck, I'm not giving credit where it is due — in God's loving care.

Blessed are the pure in heart, for they will see God (Matt. 5:8 NIV).

Thank You, Jesus, for the many blessings You give me. Humble my spirit to acknowledge that the good gifts come from You. Amen.

RIGHT OR WRONG?

In high school I started to make many of my own decisions. Mother and dad weren't always near to see what choices I made and tell me whether something was the right thing to do. I enjoyed the freedom, but along with freedom came responsibility.

Deciding what is right and wrong for a Christian can be difficult. Four guidelines a friend had written in the back of her Bible have helped me:

1. Don't go anywhere you wouldn't want to go with Jesus.

2. Don't do anything you wouldn't want to do with Jesus.

3. Don't say anything you wouldn't want to say to Jesus.

4. Don't think anything you wouldn't want to think with Jesus.

Anyone who says he is a Christian should live as Christ did (1 John 2:6 LB).

Keep instilled within me, Father, the ability to know right from wrong. Guide me in everything I do, say, or think, that all will be for Your glory. Amen.

WHY DO YOU SERVE?

I recently read a short article entitled, "Why Do You Serve?" which said: "If we serve God because we fear Him, we are slaves. If we serve God because we feel we ought to, then we are servants. But if we serve God because we love Him, we become sons and daughters."

God doesn't want me to be His slave or servant. He wants

to be my loving Father. Our relationship is determined by how I serve Him.

Say "Thank you" to the Lord for being so good, for always being so loving and kind (Ps. 107:1 LB).

Thank You for being my Father and letting me be one of Your children. You are so good. Amen.

February 12

FINDING THE FAULT OF FAULTFINDING

The title for this devotion was also the title of an editorial in our school newspaper. It really caught my eye. It's easier to find the faults of people, school, church, and community, rather than to seek out their good qualities. I was even under the impression at one time that if I wanted people to think I was really smart, I'd find what was wrong with things.

Now I'm convinced that Christ's way is to look for the good. (Although not so much to the extreme that we don't recognize the evil.) Enough people grumble about bad conditions without us, as Christians, helping them. Christ was sent into the world to bring peace and love abundantly. We are now His messengers on earth and therefore have a responsibility to let His love shine through us to others.

An optimist is more fun to be around than a faultfinder.

A person who is pure of heart sees goodness and purity in everything; but a person whose own heart is evil and untrusting finds evil in everything (Titus 1:15 LB).

I want to be like You, Jesus. I want to spread Your love and peace, instead of complaining and finding fault. With Your help I know I can do it. Amen.

LET GO

A farmer saw a cat fall into a well, and he hurried over to rescue it. When he looked down into the well, he saw that the cat was clinging to a ledge to prevent a further drop. The farmer quickly lowered a bucket into the well, but the cat wouldn't fall into it. Finally, when the cat could hold on no longer, it let go and fell into the bucket, and the farmer rescued it.

Sometimes I am like the cat. When I get myself into scary situations, God just waits for me to fall into His loving arms and leave everything up to Him so He can rescue me. Trusting God completely can be scary, but He is faithful.

I look to you for help, O Lord God. You are my refuge (Ps. 141:8 LB).

Thank You, Savior, for being close-by to rescue me from the situations I run into. I'm sorry for the times when I don't let go completely and trust You. Amen.

THE JOY OF GIVING

Two days before Valentine's Day our school exchanged names by which our "Secret Hearts" were determined. Each person was given an opportunity to do something special for the person whose name he or she had picked. On Valentine's Day shouts of joy and happy faces lined the halls and filled the classrooms as students found such things as anonymous valentines, cookies, candy, decorated lockers, balloons, cakes, and their lunches already paid for. The mood of the entire school was brightened because of these simple acts of kindness.

That day reminded me of the joy that comes from showing people I care. Valentine's Day is a great time for showing friends how much I love them, but so are the other 364 days in the year.

In response to all he has done for us, let us outdo each other in being helpful and kind to each other and in doing good (Heb. 10:24 LB).

Thank You, Father, for being so kind and for giving me the gift of kindness. Grant that I will never stifle the urge to do a favor or pass up a chance to make someone happier. Amen.

February 15

GIVE FREELY

At home, mother has a bulletin board on which she posts articles and thoughts that may be helpful or interesting to us. One week I discovered one that was both thought-provoking and challenging.

The happy ones are those who:

Give love rather than expect love.

Reach out to others rather than expecting to be reached out to.

Desire to be a friend more than to have friends.

Express appreciation rather than expect appreciation.

Love to relieve suffering rather than think of their own suffering.

Think on others' good points rather than ponder failings.

Pray "God bless others" more than "God bless me."

Give freely without thought of being given to.

Are more conscious of their neglect of others than of others' neglect of them.

Have forgotten themselves in doing things which are remembered.

Each man should give what he has decided in his heart to give, not reluctantly or under compulsion, for God loves a cheerful giver (2 Cor. 9:7 NIV).

Thank You for giving me so much, Lord. I pray that I may always be ready to give with a willing heart. Amen.

February 16

ONE STEP AT A TIME

When my brother came home from his first day in kindergarten, he announced that he wasn't going back because he hadn't learned how to read or play the piano. He didn't realize that those things take time to learn.

The same thing happens in the Christian life. We have so much to learn about our life with God that there is no end to the knowledge. Yet sometimes everything looks too complicated, and giving up looks like the easiest way out.

God doesn't expect me to learn everything at once; therefore I must trust Him as He leads one step at a time.

Do your best to present yourself to God as one approved, a workman who does not need to be ashamed and who correctly handles the word of truth (2 Tim. 2:15 NIV).

Give me patience, Lord, to follow Your leading and not look ahead to where others may be. Amen.

February 17

A CHRISTIAN — A WITNESS

Is it possible for others to know I'm a Christian by their being in school with me for a week? A month? A year? When I was asked that question, it made me think. In what ways do I let others know whom I serve? I never went witnessing door to door or passed out tracts or led a Bible study.

Then I thought about some Christian friends of mine and how they witness. I discovered they did it in many ways: by being available when a friend or neighbor is in need, or by kindness and patience when talking with people. Some Christians are preachers and teachers, while others live their faith more quietly. I am always a witness to those I come in contact with each day. To be a nonwitnessing Christian is impossible. I'm not a lesser Christian because my way of witnessing isn't the same as my brothers' and sisters'.

And how can we be sure that we belong to him? By looking within ourselves: are we really trying to do what he wants us to do? (1 John 2:3 LB).

Use me, Lord, as Your witness in whatever way You need me. Keep me ever mindful of Your presence within me so I may portray You to others. Amen.

February 18

HE'S ALWAYS NEAR

When I was small, I was afraid of the dark. Mother always told me that God was right beside me and there was no need to be afraid, but I was afraid anyway.

Recently, as a friend shared Psalm 139 with me, I began to realize in a new and real way how close God is to me all the time. I couldn't get away from Him if I wanted to! No darkness is too dark, no place too far away, no thought too secret, no action too small, to hide from God.

I find a lot of comfort in the fact that such a tremendous God is so interested in me that I can't think or do anything without His knowing! That's ultimate caring!

This is too glorious, too wonderful to believe! I can never be lost to your Spirit! I can never get away from my God! (Ps. 139:6,7 LB).

Wonderful Savior, help me to be more aware of and more thankful for Your continual presence. Amen.

HONORABLE PARENTS

"Honor your father and mother." Any time I'm tempted to disregard that command, I remind myself of these things:

- My parents, along with God, were partners in my creation.
- They spent countless hours day and night, comforting me as a crying infant, cooking for me, washing me, and just spending time with me.
- Large amounts of their money go to my care.
- They have allowed me to make many mistakes; so I should allow them to make a few too. After all, they're only human, like me.
- God commanded me to honor and obey them.

The last reminder is enough in itself. Anyone who has done as much for me as my parents have deserve my love, respect, and praise. Christ didn't say it wouldn't be difficult sometimes, but He did say to honor them.

"Honor your father and mother" — which is the first commandment with a promise — "that it may go well with you and that you may enjoy long life on the earth" (Eph. 6:2,3 NIV).

O God, thank You for such wonderful parents! Let me always be aware of them as people who love me so much that they're giving a big part of their lives for me. Amen.

SERVE TODAY

I was listening to the presentation of the Christian Young Peoples Association. They were asking for volunteers to help with retarded persons, jail visitation, young children, and people in nursing homes. The ideas all sounded good, but I decided to wait until next year, because this year would be too busy.

Then the speaker's words cut into my thoughts. He said that if our excuse is that we're too busy, that's the way it's going to be for the rest of our lives. We must begin serving the Lord today, which means making time in our schedules to do His work. God's work can't be put off!

Teach us to number our days and recognize how few they are; help us to spend them as we should (Ps. 90:12 LB).

Teach me, Lord, the wisest use of my time. May I never be too busy to serve You. Amen.

LONELINESS

Loneliness is an emotion that can spoil the good things in life for days, weeks, and even months if we let it.

I was lonely at a retreat with thirty other kids my age. I was lonely in the midst of a family who cared about me. I was lonely at school with people all around.

My dad and I were talking about the causes of loneliness. He said that often loneliness stems from self-centeredness. I began to analyze some of the times I had been lonely and found to my surprise that he was right.

My loneliness couldn't be blamed on anyone else, because each time I was done feeling sorry for myself and decided to get back into the mainstream of life, my friends were always waiting to accept me back. I must be willing to stop feeling sorry for myself long enough to see past my own selfishness.

Lord, when doubts fill my mind, when my heart is in turmoil, quiet me and give me renewed hope and cheer (Ps. 94:19 LB).

Father, thank You for showing me the causes of loneliness. With Your help, I want to reach out to others rather than think only of myself. Amen.

February 22

OVERCOMING LONELINESS

After I discovered what causes loneliness, I began to think of ways to overcome it. By admitting loneliness, I was really saying, "I can't think of anyone but myself."

Therefore, to overcome loneliness one must think of others. Ideas came to my mind such as baking something for a sick neighbor, sending a note of appreciation to a teacher, or just spending time talking to someone. After a few experiences of reaching out, I realized the truth of this cure. The joy of giving of myself to others took the lonely feelings away.

Do for others what you want them to do for you (Matt. 7:12 LB).

Lord, when I'm feeling lonely, help me to recognize my selfish attitude and get rid of it by doing something for someone else. Amen.

PLANT GOD'S WORD DEEP

The parable of the sower was always an interesting story to me, but recently a friend shared a new insight which made it more meaningful. Like the seed in the parable, I need to let God's message sink deep into my heart and produce fruit in the way I live and love others.

If, like the birds, worry and doubt enter my life and try to take away God's message, I should not try to chase the birds away; I should plant God's word deep enough in my heart that outside forces of evil don't stop my growth.

In this world, evil forces will always be present. Only when I have God's Word planted deep within can I withstand the pressure.

> **But what was sown on good soil is the man who hears the word and understands it. He produces a crop, yielding a hundred, sixty or thirty times what was sown (Matt. 13:23 NIV).**

God, I pray that Your Word will be planted so deep within me that nothing can take it away. Produce fruit in my relationships as I continue to live and love. Amen.

DON'T COMPLAIN, GIVE THANKS

A friend once told me, "If, for one day, I was in your shoes, I'd be happy." That surprised me. I hadn't realized my circumstances were that good.

After thinking about it, I realized how much I have to be thankful for that I had been taking for granted. I can't remember thanking God for my internal organs, although if I didn't have them I'd be in poor shape. It's easier to complain than to be thankful: "My nose is too long" instead of "I'm glad I can smell," "I wish I had longer legs" instead of "I'm glad I have legs."

Who am I to tell God He did a lousy job when He created me? He didn't make a mistake. He created me exactly as He wanted me. This world would be boring if everyone looked alike and had the same talents. The sooner I stop complaining and am thankful the better. Only in accepting myself can I be of any worth to Christ.

> **Always give thanks for everything to our God and Father in the name of our Lord Jesus Christ (Eph. 5:20 LB).**

My gracious Lord, thank You for making me just as I am. Guard me from any desire to change what I cannot change, but to accept myself as You made me. Amen.

February 25

BELIEVE AND OBEY

As I was reading Dietrich Bonhoeffer's book *The Cost of Discipleship*, I came across this proposition: "Only those who believe obey and only those who obey believe." Bonhoeffer went on to say that belief without obedience or obedience without belief doesn't save a man. Both are necessary.

Sometimes it's easy for me to focus all my attention on good works for salvation. Other times I think I'm saved by God's grace when I believe. But it's only when the two are working together that God can use me for His purposes.

> **As the body without the spirit is dead, so faith without deeds is dead (James 2:26 NIV).**

Savior, keep me from concentrating too much on obedience to believe and from thinking that belief without obedience is enough. Amen.

STUBBORN DOUBTS

When I have something planned, and I can see clearly how everything is going to work out, it's easy to become impatient with those who hesitate to give their cooperation because they don't understand everything completely.

That makes me wonder how God can have patience with me and with all the other stubborn creatures He lovingly calls His children. When I stop, He waits until I am willing to go on, even though He knows that if I'd only trust Him, everything would be all right. It's insulting to God to test every step when He has promised to lead me. I must put my faith in Him.

"You of little faith," he said, "why did you doubt?" (Matt. 14:31 NIV).

Praise God, who has my life mapped out for me and promises to guide and take care of me. May I leave all my stubborn doubts behind and follow You. Amen.

BEING PICKED ON?

Sometimes the whole world seems to be picking on one person — me. Strangely enough, Romans 5:3 tells us we are to rejoice if this happens because problems and trials are good for us — they teach us patience. God promises not to tempt us beyond what we can stand, but will make a way for us to escape. Out of His love for us God allows troubles, so we can become stronger in the Christian life. The growing pains help us to achieve another part of our goal to become more Christlike.

I should be concerned if I haven't had any hard times for a

while. God tests the righteous, not the wicked, so it's really a privilege to have a rough time. Then we know God's still working on us and hasn't given up.

For when he punishes you, it proves that he loves you. When he whips you it proves you are really his child (Heb. 12:6 LB).

Kind Father, thank You for wanting me as Your child. May I always have the strength and will to overcome the growing pains, so that I may be a better child for Your kingdom. Amen.

February 28

HAVING FUN WITH GOD

Becoming bogged down with my work can take all the fun out of life. I think I have so much to do that I can't take a little time off to go to a party with my friends or play the piano or even read a book just for fun.

I don't think God wants me to be that busy. If I'm always working or worrying about everything I have to do, God has to work overtime. He has to give me strength to do my work besides keeping me from becoming too run-down with worry.

When I find myself constantly worrying and working, I must give God some time off from my drudgery of work and go to a party with Him or take a walk. God likes my having fun too.

Come to me, all you who are weary and burdened, and I will give you rest (Matt. 11:28 NIV).

Thank You, Savior, for Your promise of giving me rest. I thank You that I can take time off with You to have fun. Amen.

TEACHERS — ARE THEY HUMAN?

Teachers — who are they? They're good topics to discuss and laugh about with friends. They're something to be avoided when rules are being broken. They're objects of resentment when they give homework the night of a football game. They're receivers of many unkind comments. But most important and sometimes least remembered, they're people.

After learning to know some of my teachers as friends instead of as dictators, I have been able to understand them better. Surprisingly enough, they have the same hurts, worries, and cares as every other human. Admittedly, to some teaching is only a job, but to most it's a job in which they can also help students in the best way they know how. What other job requires working far into the night on the next day's lesson plans or correcting papers? Teachers are some of the most dedicated people I know. I'm sure many times they don't feel like grading my papers any more than I feel like writing them, but they do it to help me, even if I don't always appreciate it. They deserve more praise than is given to them.

Think highly of them and give them your whole-hearted love because they are straining to help you (1 Thess. 5:13 LB).

Thank You, Jesus, for all the people who have dedicated their lives to giving me a good education.. Teach me to appreciate their work and not to take it for granted. Help me know each one as a person, not as a dictator. Amen.

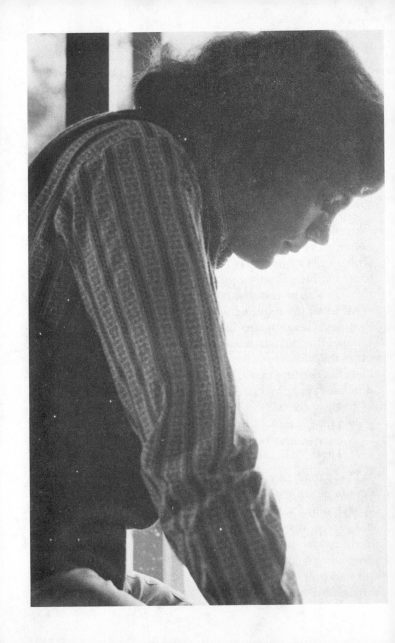

LET THERE BE . . .

In the beginning of creation God said, "Let there be light," and there was light. He said, "Let there be heavens and earth," and they appeared too.

In the beginning, whatever God commanded happened. But then man came and messed all that up.

Now God wants peace and joy, but people stand in His way. God wants to do so much with my life — all I have to do is give myself over to Him completely. Then He can say, "Let there be helpfulness," and there will be.

If I wonder why God doesn't work miracles in my life as He did in the beginning, I have to ask myself if I'm not the one at fault.

Then God said, "Let there be light." And light appeared (Gen. 1:3 LB).

Lord, let me be open to You. Work in my life and carry out Your miracles through me. Amen.

PRAISE HIM

In recent experiences, I've found that it's easy to praise God when good things are happening. The difficult time is when disaster strikes. When studies are hard and don't seem to get done, when friends seem insensitive to my needs, when a disagreement has taken place: these are times when I ask, "Why, God?" I forget that He allows good and bad times alike, and He's always with me to help me through the rough ones. Since God alone knows the future and how all my present experiences are fitting in to make the best results, I must always trust Him and thank Him for everything — even when it doesn't make sense to me.

> **For just as the sufferings of Christ flow over into our lives, so also through Christ our comfort overflows (2 Cor. 1:5 NIV).**

Lord, forgive me for times when I complain about my hardships instead of praising You. May I be content in every situation, knowing that You are in control. Thank You. Amen.

MANY MIRACLES

Two more rockets were blasted off into space, but this time I didn't watch. My great-grandparents would have watched this tremendous achievement spellbound — an achievement which has become almost commonplace for my generation.

Millions of miracles happen all around me every day, and I take them for granted. It has been said that the first time a thing occurs, it's called a miracle; later it becomes normal, and no attention is paid to it.

Worship and praise can become normal too. At rallies where everyone is talking about God's amazing love, it's easy to become spiritually high and think Christianity is the best thing. The tough part is coming back home to the regular routine again.

Worship, however, doesn't have to become routine. Each day God performs many new miracles in my life. My job is to hunt for them and continue to praise Him anew every day.

> **Don't ever forget those wonderful days when you first learned about Christ. . . . Do not let this happy**

trust in the Lord die away, no matter what happens (Heb. 10:32,35 LB).

Your greatness, almighty Savior, is far beyond anything imaginable. I humbly thank You for giving me life, a rich supply of loving friends, and the biggest miracle of all, Your Son who died for me. Amen.

March 4

GOD LEADS

"The will of God will never lead you where the grace of God cannot keep you." Those words were on a poster and they have come to have much meaning in my life.

Sometimes I feel like I'm in a situation which seems impossible to get out of. I wonder if God knew what He was doing this time. The exciting thing is that in every situation God does know, and He always works everything out in His own time and way. I don't have to doubt or fear the places God leads me because I know He will always be with me.

We live within the shadow of the Almighty, sheltered by the God who is above all gods (Ps. 91:1 LB).

Thank You, Father, for the knowledge that wherever Your will leads me, Your grace will also keep me. Amen.

March 5

THE LIGHT OF THE WORLD

Experimenting with prisms can be fun! When light shines through a prism, it's amazing how many colors there are in a beam of light.

Jesus Christ is the light of the world, yet many people

haven't seen how beautiful that light is. All facets of Christ's personality need to be shown, and the only way that can be accomplished is through His followers. The important job of shining Christ's light in all its glory to those around us is a big task, and it belongs to each of us.

Don't let anyone look down on you because you are young, but set an example for the believers in speech, in life, in love, in faith and in purity (1 Tim. 4:12 NIV).

Jesus, thank You for entrusting to me the job of being a prism for Your light. Amen.

March 6

THE MEANING OF SUCCESS

Bessie Anderson Stanley gives a good definition of success in her poem:

That man is a success
who has lived well, laughed often and loved much;
who has gained the respect of intelligent men and the
   love of children;
who has filled his niche and accomplished his task;
who leaves the world better than he found it
whether by . . .
a perfect poem or a rescued soul;
who never lacked appreciation of earth's beauty or
   failed to express it;
who looked for the best in others and gave the best he
   had.

In everything you do, put God first, and he will direct you and crown your efforts with success (Prov. 3:6 LB).

Thank You, God, for success, even though it may not be what the world would call success. Amen.

OUR FATHER

I watched a film at which we were all told to stand and repeat the Lord's Prayer together. After we said, "Our Father," we were stopped and told to sit down again.

The film went on to emphasize the fact that God is our Father and that makes us all brothers and sisters in Him. All who stood and said, "Our Father," have the same Father, even though many of us didn't know each other. Thinking about everyone as being in one family makes each person seem special and worth learning to know. Even if I'd rather not be a sister to someone, I can't disown that person, because by having the same Father, we're in the same family.

> **But you are not to be called "Rabbi," for you have only one Master and you are all brothers (Matt. 23:8 NIV).**

Father, thank You for the sense of unity I have with those around me by knowing that because of You, we're all brothers and sisters. Amen.

GROWING PAINS

Hurts, hurts, and more hurts. If I'm a Christian and God loves me as much as He says, why does He allow me to be hurt this much? This question may be asked often and may turn into bitterness if I don't keep reminding myself why God allows hurts in my life.

Being a Christian doesn't mean my misfortunes will automatically disappear. God doesn't simply move into action every time I need a miracle performed. He does what's best for me whether I realize it at the time or not.

Looking back, I can see how various hurts in my life have helped me. It's easier for me to understand what a friend is going through if I have already experienced a similar hurt. I can help that person pull through rough times by sharing my experience. Hurts can become blessings.

If all Christians were shielded against hurts, we could no longer be sensitive to non-Christians, and communication with them would be lost.

I want to learn to look for good in every situation.

Give thanks in all circumstances, for this is God's will for you in Christ Jesus (1 Thess. 5:18 NIV).

Equip me, O God, in any way You choose, to be a better servant for You, even if it means hurts. Grant me an attitude which seeks to find the good in everything, even if it takes awhile. Amen.

March 9

LISTENING TO CHRIST

Prayer and communication with God is one of the most essential parts of the Christian life, but sometimes it becomes almost meaningless. Too often my prayers are a monologue — I'm talking to God, but not listening and giving Him a chance to talk to me.

By nature, I am more eager to act and talk than to listen. I need to learn to listen, not only to others, but also to Christ. Prayer has at least two objects: talking, or thinking, and listening. I must learn to spend more time listening.

And Samuel replied, "Yes, I'm listening" (1 Sam. 3:10 LB).

Lord, forgive me when I talk too much. Teach me to listen to others and to You. Amen.

THINK

When I'm with friends, it's hard to remember that God gave me two ears and one mouth for a purpose — to listen twice as much as I talk.

Along with the urge to talk comes the tendency to talk about people who aren't around, which can be bad if it is derogatory or gossip. A friend gave me a hint to help me with this problem, and it works if I stop long enough to THINK before making a comment about anyone.

T — Is it True?
H — Is it Honest?
I — Is it Important?
N — Is it Necessary?
K — Is it Kind?

If the answer to any of these five questions is no, it most likely isn't worth saying.

Don't grumble about each other, brothers. Are you yourselves above criticism? (James 5:9 LB).

Dear Jesus, forgive me for the times I've spoken unkindly about a classmate. Help me to THINK before I talk. Amen.

THY WILL BE DONE

Too often I find myself praying as if I want God's will to be changed, instead of "Thy will be done." Jesus promises that our prayers will be heard if we ask anything according to His will, but it's not always easy to know what His will is. Sometimes we try to manipulate God or ask Him to manipulate others, so everything will turn out according to our will. Unless I'm consciously seeking God's will, it's easy to mix up my own wants with His.

We have this assurance in approaching God, that if we ask anything according to his will, he hears us (1 John 5:14 NIV).

Lord, keep me mindful of Your will. Teach me to pray according to what You want and be satisfied with that. Amen.

STRENGTH WITH CHRIST

Recently, I listened to a preacher tell a story to children. For illustration he used a toothpick, a nail, and a rubber band. The toothpick, which the children were able to break in two with no problem, represented man. The nail, which no one could begin to bend, represented God and the united body of believers. Then the preacher bound the toothpick to the nail with the rubber band, and the toothpick could no longer be bent.

I am like the toothpick. Anything can happen if I stand alone, but when I'm united with Christ and other believers, I can't be broken.

We who are strong ought to bear with the failings of the weak, and not to please ourselves (Rom. 15:1 NIV).

Thank You, Savior, for being my strength to lean on. Amen.

HOW TO BE PERFECTLY MISERABLE

I came across some steps on "How to Be Perfectly Miserable," which opened my eyes to ways I was actually making myself miserable. Some of them are;

Think about yourself.

Talk about yourself.

Use "I" as often as possible.

Mirror yourself continually in the opinion of others.

Listen greedily to what people say of you.

Expect to be appreciated.

Be sensitive to slights. Never forget criticism.

Be suspicious, jealous, and envious.

Trust nobody but yourself.

Insist on consideration and respect.

Demand agreement with your own views on everything.

Sulk if people are not grateful to you for favors shown them.

Never forget a service you have rendered.

Be on the lookout for a good time for yourself, shirk your duties if you can.

Love yourself supremely, be selfish, and do as little as possible for others.

Love . . . is not rude, it is not self-seeking, it is not easily angered, it keeps no record of wrongs (1 Cor. 13:5 NIV).

Prevent me, Father, from that selfishness which only makes me miserable. Amen.

THE OPPOSITE OF LOVE — SELF

"The opposite of love is not hate, but self. The more of self the less we can love." Those words, written in our church bulletin, made me stop and think. I had never heard it put like that before, but it's so true.

Amy Carmichael captured this thought in *If*, a book she wrote about love. "If I am afraid to speak the truth, lest I lose affection, or lest the one concerned should say, 'You do not understand,' or because I fear to lose my reputation for kindness; if I put my own good name before the other's highest good, then I know nothing of Calvary love."

Only by forgetting selfish desires can I experience love.

Create in me a new, clean heart, O God, filled with clean thoughts and right desires (Ps. 51:10 LB).

Lord, I share the prayer of the psalmist. Take away my old self and put Your Spirit in its place. Amen.

March 15

LOVE OF HUMAN PRAISE

Another mark of the self-life is the love of human praise. Often, when I've done a good job on schoolwork or a speech, or done an act of kindness, I long to be praised. If no one comments on my success, I sometimes wonder whether it was worth the effort after all.

Then I'm reminded again that longing for praise comes from selfishness. Christ received far less praise than He deserved, but His love doesn't need human praise. He continues to love.

But because of the Pharisees they would not confess their faith for fear they would be put out of the synagogue; for they loved praise from men more than praise from God (John 12:42,43 NIV).

Thank You, Father, for Your love. Teach me that Your rewards are enough for my successes and that I don't need human praise. Amen.

IMPATIENCE

A man confessed to his pastor, "I love God all right. My problem is that I don't love people."

When friends rub me the wrong way and I'm quick to react to what others say or do, then I know how immature I am in the Christian life. Impatience is sometimes excused as a sensitive spirit or nervousness, but if Christ can't be seen in my relationships to other people, practical Christianity is not present.

The test of patience is not how much I love God, but how much I love the people I come in contact with every day. Patience, one fruit of the Spirit, is cultivated and grown in my close relationships with others.

Love is patient, love is kind (1 Cor. 13:4 NIV).

Lord, increase my patience in all my relationships, even when I don't agree with everyone. Amen.

A SPIRIT OF PRIDE

Becoming wrapped up in my own world of studying, working, friends, and fun is dangerous, and it happens too often. It naturally makes what I do and think seem important, but what others do of little consequence.

This kind of selfishness, which is really pride, puts aside the love I should have for others. Only in putting myself aside is it possible to love my brothers and sisters as Christ wants me to, having confidence in them to do their best and spending my time building them up instead of building my own ego.

If you love someone you will be loyal to him no matter what the cost. You will always believe in him, always expect the best of him, and always stand your ground in defending him (1 Cor. 13:7 LB).

Master, develop in me the kind of love that puts my own desires aside for the sake of others. Amen.

A STUBBORN, ARGUING SPIRIT

A girl was asked to play the piano for church one Sunday morning, but she refused, saying she wasn't good enough. After much coaxing from the choral director, friends, and family, she consented.

This same girl might have felt unneeded or rejected if no one had asked her to play or encouraged her. The self loves to be coaxed when asked to do something, and it picks flaws when it feels unnoticed. Love doesn't think of these selfish desires.

Work happily together. Don't try to act big (Rom. 12:16 LB).

Savior, place in me the love that doesn't let stubbornness and arguing take over. Thank You for Your example of unconditional love. Amen.

FEAR

Fear of what others will think of me is also a mark of self rather than love. I can remember many instances of not expressing my opinion, not doing something, or not going somewhere, because I was afraid of the disapproval of others.

Now I know that love was the lacking ingredient. If love is present in relationships, fear is cast out.

I cannot allow fear to stand in the way of love and of standing up for the truth.

There is no fear in love. But perfect love drives out fear, because fear has to do with punishment. The man who fears is not made perfect in love (1 John 4:18 NIV).

Lord, give me more of Your love that casts out fear, so that I may live completely for You. Amen.

March 20

SPIRIT OF ENVY

As I listened to the neighborhood gang of grade school children arguing about who was the smartest, I noticed an envious spirit among them. This type of envy sometimes seems childish to teen-agers or adults, but envy is often seen in them too, in quieter or more subtle ways.

Envy is present when an unpleasant feeling or thought is the first to enter my mind at a friend's success. Envy shows up when I speak of another's failings instead of his or her virtues. Envy is most prevalent within peer groups in which everyone would like the same position or importance. Love is the only thing that can overcome envy.

Love . . . does not envy, it does not boast, it is not proud (1 Cor. 13:4b NIV).

Thank You, Father, for a love that can cast out envy. Create in me happiness for success of my friends in my peer group. Amen.

FORMALITY AND DEADNESS

From a life of living for self arises formality and dead-ness, dryness and indifference in spiritual things. When I think only of myself, the quest for ease, money, and the luxuries of life become the most important things to me. Self does not sacrifice, so as long as I remain self-centered, no love can shine through.

Real spiritual vitality cannot break forth unless I put self aside and put others first.

Now that I, your Lord and Teacher, have washed your feet, you also should wash one another's feet (John 13:14 NIV).

Lord, with Your help I want to forget myself, and give myself to others in love. Guide me in the exciting life with You. Amen.

CRITICISM IS DESTRUCTIVE

A girl in my class, whom I didn't know well, often told me my faults. Another person in my class, one of my closest friends, asked me to forgive him for bad feelings he had previously had toward me because of my actions. In both instances I had done wrong, but my reactions to the two methods of confrontation were opposite.

When the girl made her accusations, I felt she was telling me out of spite and jealousy. Instead of trying to correct my faults, I was hurt, and I added another fault to my list — that of anger toward her.

On the other hand, my friend was confessing his own faults to me so we could have a better relationship, and that's exactly what happened. Although we didn't make a habit of telling each other our faults, this situation helped bring us closer in real Christian fellowship.

That taught me a valuable lesson. It's not my duty as a Christian to constantly be telling others their faults, but to make sure I'm doing the best I can. Their enemies do a good enough job of letting them know their faults, without my helping.

Dear brothers, don't be too eager to tell others their faults, for we all make many mistakes (James 3:1 LB).

Dear Lord, show me my own faults, and help me not to look for faults in other people. Give me Your love that doesn't notice when others do wrong. Amen.

March 23

OUR UNDESERVED LOVE

The last time I read Matthew 26, a new thought hit me. When Jesus went off by Himself to pray before His death, He told his disciples to keep watch and pray with Him, but they fell asleep *three times.* They were His best friends on earth, and they didn't even stay awake to pray with Him when He was obviously filled with sorrow.

I'm sure I do things which are just as disappointing to Jesus. But His patience with me is amazing. He could so easily wipe out the earth and start over again, but He doesn't. He continues to love and care for us all through all our unfaithfulness.

Then he said to them, "My soul is overwhelmed with sorrow to the point of death. Stay here and keep watch with me" (Matt. 26:38 NIV).

Thank You, Jesus, for loving me even though I don't deserve it. Amen.

SPIRITUAL DISASTERS AT HOME

Statistics show that more than half the people killed in falls die in their own homes. The home, which should be one of the safest places, is especially dangerous. That's probably because when we are at home, we are off guard and not watching for stumbling blocks.

The same is also true of spiritual disasters. My family has been the recipient of some of my worst displays of temper, selfishness, cruelty, jealousy, neglectfulness, and carelessness. When I'm with the people I love the most, that should be all the more reason to perform in a Christlike manner and be on my guard against stumbling blocks.

He will not permit the godly to slip or fall (Ps. 55:22 LB).

Make me conscious, Father, of the need my family has to see Christlikeness in me. Amen.

MID-YEAR BLAHS

The beginning and end of a race are the easiest to run. At the beginning, I'm fresh and eager to get going, and when the end is near, my spirits are revived to help me cross the finish line. The middle part is when I feel like quitting. The going is tough, and it seems to be unending.

A school year is much the same. After a long summer vacation, my good intentions for studying hard this year are put to work.

But after a few months of this studious attitude, the mid-year blahs set in. The motives for studying hard aren't as clear any more. The work becomes boring, monotonous, and painful.

This is when having a long-term goal is helpful. Education is a means of making me into the best instrument possible for God to use in His kingdom work. Since I want to make serving God my life goal, I must take advantage of all the training I'm receiving, so I will be better equipped to tackle the job God has waiting for me.

. . . they shall run and not be weary, they shall walk and not faint (Isa. 40:31 LB).

Lord, even through the rough mid-year blahs help me to see purpose and meaning in my studies. Instill in me a determination to stick to my schoolwork and to do my best. Amen.

March 26

IDOLATRY?

We walk as pilgrims through the earth,
   With empty hands, bereft and bare;
To gather wealth were little worth —
   'Twould only burden life the more.
If men will go the way to death,
   With them we will part company;
For God will give us all we need
   To cover our necessity.

— Tersteegen

Just as God provided manna in the wilderness for the children of Israel each day, so does He provide daily for each of His children now too. If I store up possessions, I not only spoil the gift, but also myself. It can become a barrier between God and myself, because my trust, security, and God are where my treasure is. Hoarding is idolatry.

Do not store up for yourselves treasures on earth, where moth and rust destroy, and where thieves

break in and steal. . . . For where your treasure is, there your heart will be also (Matt. 6:19,21 NIV).

Lord, show me when I become too involved in my earthly possessions. Help me to keep my life as burden-free as possible. Amen.

March 27

HEAVENLY TREASURES

Jesus' words in Matthew 6:21 can be turned around to say, "Where the heart is, there shall thy treasure be also." This answers the question of what separates legitimate use from unlawful accumulation.

My heart is in whatever hinders me from loving God more than everything else. When I find myself sacrificing time and devotion to God for some earthly pleasure, that's the time to begin asking myself where my heart really is. I should be taking time to store up treasures for eternity.

But store up for yourselves treasures in heaven, where moth and rust do not destroy, and where thieves do not break in and steal (Matt. 6:20 NIV).

Make me aware, Father, when I put earthly treasures before the eternal treasures of heaven. I only want to serve You. Amen.

March 28

THE BOOK

A few weeks ago when I was looking for something to do, I picked up my Bible and began to look it over as a whole book. What a variety of things to read!

I had thought some of our laws today are strict until I

found the laws recorded for the Israelites in the Book of Leviticus. The Book of Psalms contains beautiful poetry and songs praising God — I have discovered that these psalms express my joy so well. The Old Testament books are full of stories that really happened and prophecies that are even now being fulfilled! The New Testament also contains true stories, as well as being the guide for living the best life possible.

I find it exciting that the Bible, written long ago by people in a different culture, is as up-to-date and relevant to me as tonight's newspaper.

No one else can be compared with you. There isn't time to tell of all your wonderful deeds (Ps. 40:5 LB).

O glorious God, I humbly thank You for Your gift of the Bible. It is an inspiration to me today to read about the experiences of those who followed You in the past. Amen.

March 29

GROWING CONTINUOUSLY

I once heard the Christian's walk in life compared to that of a weight lifter. A weight lifter knows the discipline of continuous untiring effort. He doesn't expect to be able to lift as many pounds as someone who has been lifting weights longer. Through continuous work, he becomes stronger and can lift more and more.

The Christian life is similar in many ways to that of a weight lifter. A newborn Christian cannot know as much as one who's been a Christian for a longer time, but by studying the Scriptures and having fellowship with other Christians and with God, he becomes stronger. Just like the weight lifter, I have to remember that a continual effort is essential for growth in the Christian life.

Then he said to them all: "If anyone would come after me, he must deny himself and take up his cross daily and follow me" (Luke 9:23 NIV).

O Master, I give You all my life to use for Your glory. Give me patience to be content where I am, but help me to always be searching for new truths. Amen.

March 30

THE VALUE OF A SMILE

It costs nothing but gives much.

It enriches those who receive without making poorer those who give.

It takes but a moment, but the memory of it sometimes lasts forever.

None is so rich or mighty that he can get along without it.

And none is so poor but that he can be made rich by it.

It creates happiness in a home, fosters good will in business, and the countersign of friendship.

It brings rest to the weary, cheer to the discouraged, sunshine to the sad, and is nature's best antidote for trouble.

It cannot be bought, begged, borrowed, or stolen, for it is something that is of no value to anyone until it is given away.

Some people are too tired to smile, so give them one of your own — since no one needs a smile so much as he who has none to give.

I shall again praise him for his wondrous help; he will make me smile again, for he is my God! (Ps. 43:5 LB).

Thank You, Lord, for smiling on me. Remind me of the importance of a simple smile when I see someone who especially needs one. Amen.

JOYFUL FACES

Robert Louis Stevenson said, "When you looked into my mother's eyes, you knew as if He had told you why God sent her into the world — it was to open the minds of all who looked, to beautiful thought." His mother's face showed her inner joy.

Faces show not only joy, but also constant worry, resentment, and discontent. My attitudes and thoughts are displayed on my face. In my youth, I determine my facial expressions for the rest of my life. It's important to be joyful — visibly.

My soul praises the Lord and my spirit rejoices in God my Savior (Luke 1:46,47 NIV).

Thank You, Father for giving me so much joy. May it show on my face as a witness for You. Amen.

WALKING THE NARROW PATH

The Bible describes the road the Christian travels as narrow. Many distractions tempt me off the path and dangers often scare me, but when I can see Jesus going ahead of me every step of the way as my leader, I can have confidence.

When I take my eyes off Jesus and look down at the path instead, I am already in danger of going astray. I must always keep my eyes fixed on Jesus. That is the only way to stay on the narrow path.

But small is the gate and narrow the road that leads to life, and only a few find it (Matt. 7:14 NIV).

Lord, keep leading me along Your narrow road, and by Your grace, I will keep following. Amen.

TIME CONSERVATION

April is always a busy month: term papers due, the class play, various school and youth group activities, and homework. So much to do, but never enough time, it seems.

Nevertheless, last April a friend and I got together for fifteen minutes or more every day to complain about everything we had to do and to worry about when we would have time to do it all. Obviously we weren't making the best use of our time; and there were more subtle ways I wasted time also, like sleeping in instead of spending a few minutes with God before I started my day.

Even in my busiest schedules, I find time to do the things I really want or need to do. God has given each of us the same number of hours per day. How I use my time is my responsibility.

> **My whole lifetime is but a moment to you. Proud man! Frail as breath! A shadow! And all his busy rushing ends in nothing (Ps. 39:5,6 LB).**

Master, let me walk with You. When I get too busy, slow me down enough to sort out my priorities in how to use my time wisely. I dedicate this April to You. Amen.

April 3

UNSELFISH LOVE

I heard the story of a rich young man who had bought a car for his brother. When he showed it to a friend, the friend said in awe, "I wish I could be a brother like that!" The expected reaction would have been, "I wish I could *have* a brother like that!" This friend's unselfish love was strong.

When I tend to become too self-centered, this story is a good reminder of the kind of love Christ wants me to have for my brothers and sisters.

> **But Zacchaeus stood up and said to the Lord, "Look, Lord! Here and now I give half my possessions to the poor" (Luke 19:8 NIV).**

Lord, thank You for Your witness of totally unselfish love. Teach me to walk in Your footsteps of love. Amen.

April 4

TRUE COMMUNION WITH CHRIST

Sometimes I find myself doing things out of habit or to look good. I don't really do them with the right motives of

Christ's love. I need to remember that if I look good but have my back on God, I'm no better than those who don't even try to look good. My relationship with Christ is what counts. No showy religious put-on is going to get me into the kingdom of heaven. Only true fellowship with Christ assures me of salvation.

Blessed are the pure in heart, for they will see God (Matt. 5:8 NIV).

Keep me close to You, Master, that I will always have my eyes on You and not just pretend to be Your follower. Amen.

SELF-ACCEPTANCE

After hearing a sermon on self-acceptance, I was discussing what the speaker said with a friend. She was under the impression that we are to think less of ourselves than we do of others. She had understood humility as always putting herself below the other person.

These two attitudes are opposites. If I always think I'm the least important, I'm focusing my thoughts on myself, constantly comparing myself to others and coming out the loser. On the other hand, a humble person is one who hardly thinks about himself at all. He rejoices when others do well instead of being depressed when he is doing poorly.

In the Gospel of Matthew, Jesus says the first and greatest commandment is to love the Lord our God with all our heart, soul, and mind. The second greatest command is to love our neighbors as much as we love ourselves. I have to ask myself how it's possible to love my neighbor if I don't love myself. But if I love myself too much and begin to put my own interests before others, then I am wrong.

Love your neighbor as yourself (Matt. 22:39 NIV).

Loving Father, guide me in Your way of humbleness, without feeling that I'm not worth as much as my brother or sister. Instill in me the knowledge that we're all the same in Your sight. Amen.

April 6

LIGHT A CANDLE

I once read a phrase that said, "It is better to light one candle than to curse the darkness." I felt as if it was speaking directly to me. I had just had the kind of day where I came closer to cursing the darkness than to lighting a candle.

I thought about how foolish I had been. When I concentrate on how bad things are going, it's impossible to see any brightness. Only when I light a candle, by thinking about everything I have to be thankful for, or by brightening someone else's day, will the darkness disappear.

You are the light of the world (Matt. 5:14 NIV).

Thank You, Lord, for Your reminder to light a candle for You. May I always remember to do that instead of cursing the darkness. Amen.

April 7

DEATH OR LIFE?

Death is a subject all of us are familiar with, whether or not it has touched the lives of those close to us. It's hard to see death as a part of life, but for a Christian it is. It isn't only an end, but also a beginning; not only a parting, but a reunion. Dying isn't locking a door; it is merely going on to a better room. And best of all, death enables a person to be in closer communion with Christ. Life on earth is like a waiting room to a huge and beautiful mansion being prepared for each of us.

Lord, help me to realize how brief my time on earth will be. Help me to know that I am here for but a moment more (Ps. 39:4 LB).

Father, when I begin to have doubts and fears about death, remind me of all the good things that can only be attained through the death of my earthly body. Amen.

THE LINE OF LIFE

In a group exercise we were each asked to draw a line representing our experiences in life. My line was quite uneven. Sometimes it went fairly high, only to drop to some unpleasant low points. That bothered me, and I was embarrassed to let anyone see my line. I didn't want them to see how unstable I was. But to my surprise, everyone else had similar lines, and some were even more uneven. Some adults in the group, whom I thought were able to keep the ups and downs of life at a rather even pace, showed the opposite to be true by their lines.

After this experience I realized that everyone, being human, has good times, bad times, and in-between times, and that's not wrong. It makes life interesting and exciting. If I didn't have discouraging times, I wouldn't be able to appreciate the good times as much. The important thing to remember is that no matter what kind of mood I'm in, God is with me. He helps me through the rough spots and makes the good times even better.

Give your burdens to the Lord. He will carry them (Ps. 55:22 LB).

Thank You, Jesus, for going with me through each mood and helping me to make the best of every situation. Your presence is comforting. Amen.

A TIME TO RISK

A lobster must shed its old shell many times in order to grow. After each shedding, it is completely defenseless until the new shell forms.

A similar risk is present when people change. Any change produces uncertainty. But without the uncertainty, no change or opportunities are available. Like the lobster, I must be willing to take the risk of vulnerability as the price for growth.

> **Yes, be bold and strong! Banish fear and doubt! For remember, the Lord your God is with you wherever you go (Josh. 1:9 LB).**

Remind me, Father, of Your continuous watch over me. I know that with You I'll never be defenseless. Amen.

VICTORY OVER TEMPTATION

A shopping trip when I'm not looking for anything special is my downfall. I usually seem to find something that would be nice to set in my room, a good bargain on an item I've *always* wanted, beautiful material I can't possibly pass by, or a new kind of cologne. In such an affluent society, when I have money, it's hard to deny myself things I'd like to have.

In 1 Corinthians, Paul warns against idol worship. At first glance that's an easy verse to accept — it can't be so hard to follow. But maybe I do have idols. Spending my money on things I want but don't really need, instead of letting God use it for His purposes, can be idol worship. Time, money, or anything I think of before God, is an idol.

Only Christ can help me overcome this love for other things.

No temptation has seized you except what is common to man. And God is faithful; he will not let you be tempted beyond what you can bear. But when you are tempted, he will also provide a way out so that you can stand up under it (1 Cor. 10:13 NIV).

Thank You, God, for the promise that You will help me in all my temptations. Thank You too for the assurance that You won't tempt me with more than I can take. Amen.

April 11

LOVE SHARES

Susan Polis Schulz wrote the following thought for a greeting card:

Your heart is my heart;
Your truth is my truth;
Your feeling is my feeling;
But the real strength of our love,
Is that we share rather than control
Each others' lives.

True love is not possessive. The only way I can really love is to accept another person as he is and allow him to make his own decisions. When I give each relationship to God, He will guide me in sharing the other person's life without the need to control it.

I know whom I have believed, and am convinced that he is able to guard what I have entrusted to him for that day (2 Tim. 1:12 NIV).

Thank You, God, for Your perfect love. Give me more of Your loving Spirit as I seek to share rather than control others' lives. Amen.

I NEED GOD

A friend shared with me how God continually shows him weaknesses in his life just when he begins to feel that he's on top of everything. He related how this humbled him to see his need of God once again.

Since that time, I've noticed God working the same way in my life. When I become self-confident and forget God, He soon shows me who's in control.

God must be tired of my trying to get credit for His work. I need to keep reminding myself that anything I achieve is through Christ's power and not my own.

And don't think you know it all! (Rom. 12:16 LB).

Forgive me, Jesus, when I forget You. Give me weakness to keep me mindful of my need for You. Amen.

HORIZONS OF LOVE

Looking out across the land at the wide horizons is a peaceful experience for me. It reminds me of God's love. I can't even imagine the expanse of His love. If I'd go to one horizon, another would lie ahead. There will always be another horizon, wherever I go, just as God's love will always surround me.

That's the kind of love Christians are told to have for each other. A love that is always present. A love that has no end. A love that holds up no matter what happens. A love that doesn't disappear with unpleasant circumstances. A love that is peaceful and beautiful forever.

If you love those who love you, what reward will you get? Are not even the tax collectors doing that? . . . Be

perfect, therefore, as your heavenly Father is perfect (Matt. 5:46,48 NIV).

Thank You, God, for showing me how infinite Your love is. Give me the same love for all my brothers and sisters. Amen.

LISTEN IN SILENCE

It's a misty evening as the rain falls softly. The sun has been down for awhile, but it's still light enough to see a little. That's my favorite setting for a quiet walk and talk alone with God.

Being with others is enjoyable and necessary, but in all the activity, sometimes I forget the necessity of being alone with God. At those times God must feel like telling me to slow down, be quiet, and listen to Him for awhile. But He patiently waits for me to realize it on my own, and when I'm ready, He's there waiting for me.

Being silent and listening to God and His creation is rewarding. It's amazing how many different sounds can be heard. Above all, it's amazing what God has to tell me when I become still and am willing to listen to Him.

Stand silent! Know that I am God! (Ps. 46:10 LB).

Thank You, Father, for being so patient with me, one of your creatures who sometimes doesn't even stop to listen to her Creator. You're so wonderful – I want to be with You forever. Amen.

THE RIGHT TRAIN?

I see life as two trains, with everyone in one or the other. The trains are going in opposite directions and each person may choose which one he wants to ride. No one is at a standstill. Each person must be going in one of the two directions.

God's train doesn't have as many seats, but the scenery is better. It's harder to hang onto, but when the destination is kept in sight, the extra effort is worth it. The beautiful fact is that God always welcomes new passengers, and He loves them just as if they'd been on His train the whole time. Why would I ever want to be on the train going away from God?

For I did not come to judge the world, but to save it (John 12:47 NIV).

Lord, I'm so glad I'm on Your train. Thank You for reserving a seat for me. Amen.

April 16

GROW IN THE LORD

Peanuts have a unique and interesting way of growing. When the blossoms have been pollinated, the stalk bends down and goes beneath the ground. The peanuts then grow underground to ripeness and become useful for many things.

I also bow before God and develop in Christ, together with other members of His body. When He brings me to maturity, I am most useful to Him.

But grow in the grace and knowledge of our Lord and Savior Jesus Christ (2 Peter 3:18 NIV).

O God, my Creator, thank You for teaching me how to be useful on earth. Amen.

April 17

DO THOUGHTS MATTER?

Recently I read, "Be careful what you think, what you listen to, what you do. It is placed forever in the memory." I knew that what I listen to and what I do are important, but how about what I think? Is that just as crucial for living the best possible Christian life? It was a new thought and I didn't know how to answer my own question.

A few Sundays later I heard a sermon that barely touched on the subject, but it gave me a clue that the answer is in the Bible.

What I found surprised me. In Philippians, Paul tells us in the name of Christ what to think about. Since God has commanded me to control my thinking, He must have given me the power to control it. Some things are difficult to keep out of my mind, but I know that with Jesus helping me, I can forget them. If I fill my thoughts with those things God commands me to think about, the impure thoughts disappear.

Finally, brothers, whatever is true, whatever is noble, whatever is right, whatever is pure, whatever is lovely, whatever is admirable — if anything is excellent or praiseworthy — think about such things (Phil. 4:8 NIV).

Lord Jesus, I confess that I haven't done my best at keeping my thoughts pure. Forgive me, and help me to start today to control my thinking for Your sake. Amen.

April 18

MORE ON THINKING

Recently I ran across a saying that caused me to do more thinking on the importance of my thought life:

Sow a thought, and you reap an act;
Sow an act, and you reap a habit;
Sow a habit, and you reap a character;
Sow a character, and you reap a destiny.

— Anonymous

My thoughts are crucial to the well-being of my spiritual life. What I think is what I eventually become.

Some time ago a preacher told us to think of every dirty word we knew of and then ask God to keep those words out of our minds. But as I understand Christ, He doesn't tell us that the way to overcome evil thoughts is to constantly battle them. Rather, my primary concern should be to cultivate good thinking. I am to exert every mental effort to think about things that are good and pure.

This means guarding against things which pollute my mind. Instead I should help it to attain only pure thoughts. Each area of life is so important for living totally for Christ that I must not think that one part — my thought life — doesn't make any difference. It will determine my destiny.

Keep a close watch on all you do and think (1 Tim. 4:16 LB).

Strengthen in me, Lord, the power to cultivate pure thoughts. Guide me in all phases of life that I might think only that which will be for Your glory. Amen.

April 19

PART OF THE TRUTH

The parable Buddha told of the blind men and an elephant is interesting. Each of the ten blind men were to touch one part of the elephant and report their conclusions. An argument soon began because each man thought the part he touched was a different animal.

Buddha said that is how men view truth. Too often I think that the little bit of truth I know is the whole truth. But people who have different ideas from mine aren't necessarily wrong. They may just have a different part of the truth.

As an Indian sage said in a parable about mountain climbers: "You don't get the view from the foot of the mountain. It is only from the top, you see the whole picture."

For we know in part and we prophesy in part, but when perfection comes, the imperfect disappears (1 Cor. 13:9,10 NIV).

Thank You for being patient with me, Lord, as I seek the truth. Give me patience and understanding for others' concept of truth. Amen.

April 20

AMEN

Recently a friend related to me an experience of his, in which after praying with a friend, they didn't say "Amen," because they felt God was still with them. They didn't want to turn Him off with a hasty "Amen."

Too many times, a quick "Amen" finishes a prayer, signifying one task done and readiness to move on to something else. I have to be careful that my "Amen" doesn't stop my communication with Jesus but is an incentive to continue it.

Amen. Come, Lord Jesus (Rev. 22:20 NIV).

I want You to be with me continually, Jesus. May my "Amen" be not one of finality, but one of beginning the experiences I have to share with You. Amen.

April 21

THE ASSURANCE OF SALVATION

At one point in my life I didn't know whether or not I'd go to heaven if Jesus came back before the next morning. It bothered me but I didn't feel I could tell anyone, because as a professing Christian, I supposedly had the assurance of my salvation.

I had accepted Christ as my Savior and asked Him to be Lord of my life, but sometimes I had doubts. Then I'd ask Him to come into my life again, just in case He hadn't already.

This was a miserable state of mind, so I was glad when I received some help. I heard a preacher say that to be saved I merely needed to accept Jesus, ask Him to be Lord of my life, and then believe that He lives in me. To invite Jesus into my life more than once is actually an insult to Him, saying that I don't believe He took my first invitation.

Now, as I keep turning over new areas of my life to Christ, I am conscious all the time that I'm saved, and He is preparing a place for me in heaven.

For the Son of Man came to seek and to save what was lost (Luke 19:10 NIV).

Lord, thank You for living within me and being the Lord of my life. Forgive me for ever doubting Your saving power. Amen.

April 22

BOUND BY LOVE

Westwood Purkiser said, "We can walk in fellowship with God with wrong ideas in our heads, but not with wrong attitudes in our hearts."

I like that. I have many friends who don't share exactly my opinions on everything about our lives under Christ's lordship. I'm glad, though, that we can be brothers and sisters under the same Father, even with our differences. The most important thing is for each of us to be acting upon what we truly believe God wants of us. We are bound together by His love.

Anyone is my brother who fears and trusts the Lord and obeys him (Ps. 119:63 LB).

Thank You, Father, for uniting me with Your other followers because of our common commitment to You. Amen.

MAKE A JOYFUL NOISE TO THE LORD

The choir I was in during high school combined with nine other school choirs once a year to sing together. These spine-tingling experiences are unforgettable, and I'm sure God enjoyed the beautiful music we made for Him as much as we did. It made me think of how grand and glorious it will be when we sing to our great God with all the angels of heaven .

What I couldn't understand were some of the faces in the audience and choirs. They looked as if we were marching into the worst place possible instead of marching upward to Zion, the beautiful city of God. They didn't seem to comprehend the words, "Rise! Shine! Give God the glory, children of the Lord," or "Clap your hands, all ye people."

Often congregational singing lacks enthusiasm too. We can't possibly understand the words and at the same time look like we're attending Christ's funeral, rather than celebrating His resurrection. I, along with the rest of God's people, need to pay more attention to the words we're singing and let our faces reflect the message.

I will sing to the Lord as long as I live. I will praise God to my last breath! May he be pleased by all these thoughts about him, for he is the source of all my joy (Ps. 104:33,34 LB).

"O, for a thousand tongues to sing my great Redeemer's praise, the glories of my God and King, the triumphs of his grace." Thank You for the tongue I have to use for You. Amen.

START JUMPING

Some time ago, a man shared this story in our Sunday morning service. His daughter asked him repeatedly to put her on top of the refrigerator and count to three, so she could jump. He did what she asked, but she never jumped.

He went on to relate this incident to his spiritual life. He repeatedly asks God to show him areas in his life that need to be worked on, but when God does show him, he's afraid to jump in and start working.

That's a real challenge to me to start jumping for Christ — not only for my own good, but also so others can see what He means to me and maybe do some jumping themselves!

Remember, therefore, what you have received and heard; obey it, and repent (Rev. 3:3 NIV).

Forgive me, Lord, for all the times You've said "Jump" and I've continued to sit still. Give me the courage to start the work You have for me. Amen.

TRUST IN GOD

Recently a group of us were visiting at the home of another friend for a weekend. Our friend also had a blind guest visiting. He didn't talk much, but I could tell he was listening closely to everything around him. I was not aware, however, how much he was learning. He didn't let his blindness keep him uninvolved. By the end of the first evening, he was able to tell what kind of a person each of us was, what color our eyes were, and how tall and heavy each person was. With few exceptions, he described each of us accurately.

It made me stop and think about how little I'm aware of those around me. Many times I think too much about myself instead of looking to others. I was also reminded to place more trust in God when I think I can take care of myself.

Many blessings are given to those who trust the Lord (Ps. 40:4 LB).

Teach me, Lord, to put my trust in You when I tend toward over-confidence in myself. Thank You for Your protection even when I don't fully appreciate it. Amen.

April 26

GLORIFY LIFE IN CHRIST

During high school I listened to many speakers tell about their lives before they became Christians. Some spent their entire speeches telling all the horrible situations they had been involved in and warning against trying any of them.

It seemed to me that time is better spent talking about what Christ has done for us and the kind of rewarding lives we have when we live for Him. Instead of spending time telling about bad experiences, we should concentrate on the good.

Don't envy violent men. Don't copy their ways (Prov. 3:31 LB).

Dear Jesus, thank You that I don't have a terrible past life to remember or scars to bear. Grant that I won't try to win others for Christ by showing them how awful life without Christ can be, but by letting them see how wonderful life with Christ is. Amen.

THE TIME IS NOW

Margaret Storm Jameson, an English novelist, has said: "Most of us spend fifty-eight minutes an hour living in the past with regret for lost joys, or shame for things badly done, or in a future which we either long for or dread."

That's a lot of time to think about things that don't have an effect on changing our circumstances now! Each minute is an unrepeated miracle. I should make the best use of each miracle God has given to me.

> **Be very careful, then, how you live — not as unwise but as wise, making the most of every opportunity, because the days are evil (Eph. 5:15,16 NIV).**

Thank You, Lord, for each minute. May I make the most of each miracle for Your glory. Amen.

THE STEP OF FAITH

One time a friend shared the story of Peter walking on the water, with a different emphasis than I had heard before. Too often the only thing we remember is that Peter began to sink because he didn't have enough faith.

We sometimes forget that Peter was the only one to make the attempt. All the other disciples stayed within the safety of the boat. Peter took the step of faith, without stopping to consider the possible danger. I, too, need to step out in faith, as Peter did, when the Lord tells me to come.

"Come," he said. Then Peter got down out of the boat and walked on the water to Jesus (Matt. 14:29 NIV).

Lord, thank You for Peter's example of faith. May I always be ready to answer Your call with that kind of faith. Amen.

JUDGE NOT

A friend once told me that before becoming a follower of Jesus, it was easier for her to accept others as they were. Now her temptation was to be critical and think less of others.

I must learn to love as Christ loved. He spent a lot of time with sinners, loving them. I should want to show others His kind of love, rather than looking down on them for not knowing about it or misunderstanding it.

Do not judge, or you too will be judged (Matt. 7:1 NIV).

Thank You, Father, for Your infinite love. Guide me in sharing it, with an uncritical attitude, with those around me. Amen.

PRAYER POWER

After praying about something for a long time, my friend told me she had given up on God because He didn't answer her. Sometimes I feel like giving up, too, but looking at my friend's situation helped me to better understand God's way of answering prayer.

Just because God doesn't answer all my prayers the way I think He should doesn't mean He doesn't care about me. It probably shows that He cares more by answering in the way that will be the best for me in the end, even though I don't understand now.

Too often I want immediate action to my prayers, but He sometimes answers "no" or "not yet." The test of faith is in whether or not I'm willing to accept His answer and thank Him for it even if I don't understand it.

> **Don't be weary in prayer; keep at it; watch for God's answers and remember to be thankful when they come (Col. 4:2 LB).**

Heavenly Father, thank You for hearing my prayers. Give me patience to wait for Your answer and the power to accept it with thanksgiving if it's not exactly what I was hoping for. Amen.

STRENGTH THROUGH PROBLEMS

The following statement of Robert H. Schuller has a lot to say. It is an affirmation to be remembered with each new problem.

"I will be a different person when this problem is past. I will be a wiser, stronger, more patient person; or I will be sour, cynical, bitter, disillusioned, and angry. It all depends on what I do with this problem. Each problem can make me a better person or a worse person. It can bring me closer to God, or it can drive me away from God. It can build my faith or it can shatter my faith. It all depends on my attitude. I intend to be a better person when this problem leaves me than I was when it met me."

Be joyful in hope, patient in affliction, faithful in prayer (Rom. 12:12 NIV).

Lord, thank You for showing me that my attitude determines what my problems make of me. Guide me in handling them. Amen.

TRUSTWORTHY

Last year, through many FBI investigations, the police in a neighboring town were found guilty of numerous unsolved robberies.

This reminded me once again how unstable things on earth are. I can understand why anyone who didn't have the eternal hope of heaven to hold onto could become frightened by what's happening in the world. It makes me thankful to have Jesus as my personal Friend, who promises to take care of me, even though nothing around me seems worth trusting.

Fear not, for I am with you. Do not be dismayed. I am your God. I will strengthen you; I will help you; I will uphold you with my victorious right hand (Isa. 41:10 LB).

Dear Jesus, I don't know what I'd do without You! Life would be meaningless. Thank You for being with me always. Amen.

DISCOVER HIDDEN TALENTS

All people have within themselves fantastic amounts of talent waiting to be used and developed. The sad thing is that I, along with others, fail to uncover these talents, so they remain hidden.

When I'm tempted to think God must have missed me when He was handing out talent, I need to remind myself of the parable in Scripture in which three servants were each given a different number of talents. The two who had the most made good use of them and were given more according to their ability. The servant with one talent buried it, and in the end it was taken from him.

God has given me talents, but unless I make good use of them, they will be worthless and won't produce anything for the kingdom. Maybe the person who seems to be blessed with many talents is merely making good use of the ones he has. I can overcome jealousy by discovering my own talents and developing them for God's glory.

His master replied, "Well done, good and faithful servant! You have been faithful with a few things; I will put you in charge of many things. Come and share your master's happiness!" (Matt. 25:23 NIV).

Kind Father, thank You for giving me talents. Forgive me for complaining about what I don't have instead of developing what I do have. Amen.

GET MOVING!

When my brother and I had finally mastered the art of controlling a canoe, we were quite proud of ourselves. We could go fast, stop, or move in any direction. We also learned that it's easier to turn a canoe around when it's moving than when it's stopped.

My Christian life must keep moving too. If I'm at a standstill, God has a hard time changing my direction when He needs to. He can work His will more easily in my life when I'm moving, redirecting me when necessary.

To him who overcomes and does my will to the end, I will give authority over the nations (Rev. 2:26 NIV).

Direct my ways, O God, as I travel through the waters of life. Give me strength to keep moving. Amen.

FOCUS ON JESUS

At a park near where I once lived, my favorite plaything was a huge wooden barrel. It lay on its side and three people could stand in it comfortably. By walking forward, then running, we could make the barrel turn.

Sometimes it turned so fast that we fell. A helpful technique we soon learned was to focus on something that was stable outside the barrel. By keeping our perspective in that way, we didn't become dizzy as fast.

In life, it's easy for me to become upset with the turn of events that continually arise. At those times the best thing to do is to focus on Jesus as my stability. He will keep me from becoming caught up in the whirl of activity.

Let us fix our eyes on Jesus, the Pioneer and Perfector of our faith (Heb. 12:2 NIV).

Dear Jesus, thank You for being my stabilizer in a world that moves so fast. Grant me wisdom to keep my eyes on You. Amen.

BUILDING LIFE WITH CHRIST

I remember that a few years ago a new church building was being built in our town. It seemed like a long time before the framework was finished. The building process, however, was only the beginning of the church program. The church then used the building to go on to bigger and better programs.

I see life in somewhat the same way as the building. God is the architect and contractor, and He has my life planned out already. He slowly adds more walls and rooms as I'm ready for them, but the building is never finished. I need to keep cooperating with God to build bigger and better programs into my life.

Being confident of this, that he who began a good work in you will carry it on to completion until the day of Christ Jesus (Phil. 1:6 NIV).

I thank You, God, for being the perfect Architect. I am Yours to shape and build in whatever ways You know to be best. Amen.

CONCENTRATION

Many times, during school especially, it became evident to me that my ability of concentration was lacking. It's easy for me to let my mind wander and become involved in something else before I'm finished with what I'm doing.

Then I found two things that make concentration easier. One is to have a long-term goal to work toward, and the other is to be really interested in what I'm involved in.

For example, homework can be boring and seem like a waste of time, but when I think of it as a necessary step in educating myself to become what God wants me to be, homework becomes more worthwhile to me.

The same concentration is necessary for growing in my Christian life. It's hard to be kind to people who are unkind to me and to love the unlovable, but when the rewards of Jesus' love are kept in sight, it is worthwhile.

> **Keep your eyes on Jesus, our leader and instructor. He was willing to die a shameful death on the cross because of the joy he knew would be his afterwards; and now he sits in the place of honor by the throne of God. If you want to keep from becoming fainthearted and weary, think about his patience as sinful men did such terrible things to him (Heb. 12:2,3 LB).**

Be with me, Jesus, as I live my life on earth in preparation for my life in heaven. Keep within me the long-term view of everything I do. Amen.

May 8

I SHALL PASS

Each day is new. It will last exactly twenty-four hours and then it will be gone forever. If I waste a day, I can never make it up.

Etienne de Grellet wrote a poem which is sometimes read at graduation ceremonies, but it's also a good reminder for every day:

> I shall pass through this world but once;
> Any good therefore that I can do,

Or any kindness that I can show to any fellow
  creature,
Let me do it now;
Let me not defer or neglect it,
For I shall not pass this way again.

**Satisfy us in our earliest youth with your lovingkind-
ness, giving us constant joy to the end of our lives (Ps.
90:14 LB).**

*Thank You, Father, for each new day. Help me to spend each
one in a way that will be pleasing to You. Amen.*

May 9

THE RIVER OF LIFE

As I sat on the bank of a river winding through the Virginia mountains, I saw the water as symbolizing my life.
Like the water, flowing continually even though it doesn't
know its destination or what's around the next bend, I can't
see far ahead in my life. I have to trust God to guide my
path.

The falls in the river are like the rough areas in my life.
When I'm faced with rough situations, they sometimes
look unbearable. But when seen as part of the whole, they
add beauty and sparkle to my life.

Inlets of water along the shore, at a standstill, had collected scum and debris. Again, I compared them to my life.
If I don't keep moving along God's path, my life will get
cluttered. The river of life is too exciting to refuse its flow.

**And whatever you do, whether in word or deed, do it
all in the name of the Lord Jesus, giving thanks to
God the Father through him (Col. 3:17 NIV).**

*Thank You, Lord, for controlling the flow of my life. Teach
me to follow even when I don't know what is waiting around the
next bend. Amen.*

MY LIFE — GOD'S MASTER PLAN

High school days can be the beginning of an entire life spent feeling uneasy about the future. Even though some can't wait to finish, school provides temporary security. A whole new world and many new experiences await the graduate. Anything new can be scary or exciting, depending on how we view life.

Sometimes I wish I could look into my future and see what I'll be doing in a few months or years. Then I could just make those decisions which would bring about my future without waiting to see what will happen.

That might be easier, but it would be much less exciting. If I knew about some of the good things that await me, I might get bored with life now. Or I might not be as willing to go on with life if I knew some of the disappointments my future holds.

God has chosen to keep my future a mystery to me and lead me one step at a time. I've found this to be the most exciting way to live. Knowing that God has a master plan for my life, and enjoying each new revelation to its fullest, is the most rewarding way to live.

> **Since the Lord is directing our steps, why try to understand everything that happens along the way? (Prov. 20:24 LB).**

Eternal Father, it's comforting to know that You hold my life in Your hands. Thank You for taking care of my future so I don't have to worry about it. Amen.

GOD HURTS TOO

One time I was hurt because a person I loved deeply was turning her back on God. At first I was so wrapped up in self-pity and wondering how I could help that I almost completely left God out of the picture, except to complain about how much it hurt me.

Then I thought about how much God loves each one of His children. Since His capacity to love is much greater than any human's, His hurt was deeper than I'll ever experience. He has much more to be hurting over too — each one of His children who has gone astray brings Him grief.

But God demonstrates his own love for us in this: While we were still sinners, Christ died for us (Rom. 5:8 NIV).

Lord, forgive me when I think only of myself and blame You for my hurts, forgetting all the hurts You have. Amen.

JESUS AS THE GUIDE

A family decided to go on a camping trip. They spent many weeks making plans and getting ready for it. The day of departure finally arrived, but they couldn't go because they had lost the map.

Life without Jesus as guide is much the same. I can spend a lot of time talking, reading, and thinking about the journey; but nothing is of value, unless I start out with Jesus as my guide.

I am but a pilgrim here on earth: how I need a map — and your commands are my chart and guide. I long for your instructions more than I can tell (Ps. 119:19,20 LB).

"Guide me, O thou great Jehovah, pilgrim through this barren land; I am weak, but thou art mighty; hold me with thy powerful hand." Amen.

OPEN UP TO LOVE

When the first guy I ever really fell for suddenly dropped me, I was crushed and for a long time refused to give of myself to anyone. To share deeply of my feelings again was too great a risk.

I felt that if I didn't really love a person, that when they left the hurt wouldn't be as deep and hard to deal with. This sometimes meant finding faults with friends so I wouldn't let myself grow too attached to them.

Some time later at a youth rally, I had a chance to talk with the main speaker. He told me that hurt is as much a part of life as joy, love, and the other emotions, if not more. If I don't leave myself open for occasional hurts, I won't be able to be loved either.

After thinking over that new idea, I realized that I had closed myself to the love of my friends. I had many friendships, but not on a deep, personal, sharing level. I found that life can have a much richer meaning when I'm willing to open my true self to others. It's scary but well worth it!

And to know this love that surpasses knowledge — that you may be filled to the measure of all the fullness of God (Eph. 3:19 NIV).

Lord, thank You for showing me how rich the joys of life can be when I become willing to let others know the real me. Amen.

REPORT FOR DUTY

While listening to a sermon by David Seamans, a professor at Asbury College in Kentucky, I was struck by the following statement: "Don't give God instructions — just report for duty." Sometimes I don't go to God for instructions until after I've already decided what I want. Then I ask for God's approval of my plans. I should, instead, ask my Master about His will first, then adapt my plans to fit His. This should be the normal way of living, not an extra favor that I do for God.

> **So you also, when you have done everything you were told to do, should say, "We are unworthy servants; we have only done our duty" (Luke 17: 10 NIV).**

Master, I want to report for duty today and every day. Forgive me for the times I give the instructions instead of asking for them. Amen.

May 15

ARGUING

On a trip our class took to Boston, I spent an evening at the Boston Commons. It is a park where people gather to talk about anything they want to. If anyone disagrees, they begin arguing openly. Soon a small crowd gathers around to listen and some join in.

After some observation, I noticed that even though these people might have believed what they were saying, they were arguing mostly for the enjoyment of arguing! They didn't care whom they argued with. It almost seemed to be a form of entertainment.

It made me wonder what Jesus would do if He were in that situation, and I didn't think He'd be participating. So I didn't join the arguers, but I began to think of the many times I have argued about tiny, insignificant matters. By observing others, I realized how silly my own arguments are.

> **Do everything without complaining or arguing (Phil. 2:14 NIV).**

Lord, too often I find myself caught in the trap of arguing. Grant that I will act in a Christlike manner instead. Amen.

LIVING THE NOTES

A friend of mine thought of an analogy in which he compared singing to living with God. God is like my diaphragm from which I need constant support to sing. When the notes rise, I need an extra push, just as I need extra strength from God when times become hard. To produce the best musical sound, the vocal chords must be kept free, not tightened. I, also, must remain free to let God play whatever tune He wants to with my life. To produce the right intonation, God must be my support in every "phrase" of my life.

Holiness is forever the keynote of your reign (Ps. 93:5 LB).

Thank You, God, for Your support in hitting the high, low, and in-between notes of life. Keep playing Your song in me. Amen.

SPRING OF LIFE

Youth is the springtime of life. Spring is the time for plowing under the old sod and starting anew. It's a time to go barefoot and experience new things, a time to chase butterflies and explore new places. Spring has a fresh smell and excitement in the air, just waiting to waken the world to a glorious awareness of being alive.

Spring is the time for sowing seeds that will be harvested later in life. Acts of beauty will produce good fruit. Seeds of discord will yield bad fruit. Now is the time to decide what kind of fruit I want my life to bring forth.

Flee the evil desires of youth, and pursue righteousness, faith, love and peace, along with those who call on the Lord out of a pure heart (2 Tim. 2:22 NIV).

Thank You, Father, for the spring of my life. Guide me in sowing the seeds for the fruit You want to produce in me. Amen.

INFERIORITY COMPLEX

Everyone knows what it is to have an inferiority complex and everyone has one in some area. How does this attitude start? If it's normal, why do I feel so alone?

It begins with the self-image I develop in my mind. This picture I have of myself affects my appearance, speech, and actions to a large extent. I, like everyone else, know what it's like to fail at something, and I know the damage it can do to self-confidence. This often tends to make me afraid to try again because I'm afraid of repeated failure or of what others will think of me.

Since we all have inferiority complexes, how to get rid of them is important. First, I have to be honest with myself. Pretending I'm not interested in something or being too busy are excuses I make for not trying. Next, I have to change the picture I have of myself. I have nothing better to look to but myself unless I allow God to help. With God's help, I have all the power I need. God loves me just as much as any person I'm tempted to feel inferior to.

I can do everything through him who gives me strength (Phil. 4:13 NIV).

When I feel inferior to others, Father, let me be reminded of Your ever-present love for me. With Your help, I can do all things. Thank You. Amen.

HANDLING VICTORY

Yesterday I thought about overcoming defeat, but then I realized that victory can be just as hard to handle. When I finally have the verse ingrained in me that says, "I can do everything in him," then I can think of God and myself as partners. Danger begins, however, after I gain victory. It becomes easy to leave God out and change from having confidence in God to having confidence in self.

A superiority complex and an inferiority complex are opposite extremes of the same frame of mind. I ask God for help and then take credit for what He does. I wouldn't like a friend doing that to me. These two verses must go together: "I can do everything in him" and "Apart from me you can do nothing." Victory can be a great ego-builder if God isn't given the credit for all my accomplishments.

Knowing how good the feeling of victory or accomplishment is gives me a glimpse of how pleased God is to receive the credit. He deserves it.

Don't be conceited, sure of your own wisdom. Instead, trust and reverence the Lord (Prov. 3:7 LB).

Lord, may I always give You the credit for things we do together. I know that without You I can do nothing. Amen.

PRAYER POWER

A study of the four Gospels shows how prayer was the underlying vein of Christ's whole ministry. He lived, healed, taught, raised the dead, fed, and evangelized by prayer. He even died by prayer.

In the complexity of life, I tend to plan everything, taking as many shortcuts as possible. No shortcuts exist, however, in the power of prayer. I will be of little use to Christ unless I learn to pray and witness as He taught His disciples. Just as He was given no other way, neither am I given any other way.

This is how you should pray:
"Our Father in heaven,
hallowed be your name . . ." (Matt. 6:9 NIV).

Keep me mindful, Lord, of the fact that prayer is the only way to be Your disciple. No shortcuts are available. Amen.

GUEST OR HOST?

When Christ first entered my life, I was the host and He was my guest, because I had invited Him. Soon, however, the roles had to switch. Christ became the host and I became His guest. I no longer have the right to ask anyone else in or to tell Him what to do. He is setting the example that I am to follow. To keep our roles in mind, I need to continually ask myself: Is Christ resident or president in my life? Is He a rumor or ruler?

Here I am! I stand at the door and knock. If anyone hears my voice and opens the door, I will go in and eat with him, and he with me (Rev. 3:20 NIV).

Thank You, gracious Host, for allowing me to be Your guest. May I always remember that You're my Ruler. Amen.

THE BEAUTY OF A SUNRISE

Early one morning I climbed a hill with a few of my friends to watch the sunrise. Since it was my first time to witness this exciting event, I didn't know exactly what to expect. The sky was light for at least an hour before the sun first appeared over a distant mountain. Then it quickly rose into full view within a few minutes.

It reminded me of God's presence in my life. Sometimes His presence is more visible than other times, but He's always there. The beauty of the rising sun made me hope that I can be an instrument for God's kindness at every opportunity, so others can experience and know it too.

> **Every morning tell him, "Thank you for your kindness," and every evening rejoice in all his faithfulness (Ps. 92:2 LB).**

Thank You, Creator, for the reminder of Your presence in the beauty of a sunrise. May I always serve You by letting Your love shine through me. Amen.

PRAYER IN JESUS' NAME

I had heard people end their prayers with "In Jesus' name," and I say it often myself. But until recently I didn't understand the meaning behind the phrase.

In reading through a few commentaries on the Gospel of John, I found that names in Bible times had more meaning than the spoken letters. A person's name stood for that person's entire being — his manners, personality, beliefs, actions, and thoughts. Now when I pray or praise in Jesus' name, I know I'm relating to the person of Jesus, not merely to the five-letter word.

> **I will cause your name to be honored in all generations; the nations of the earth will praise you forever (Ps. 45:17 LB).**

Jesus, thank You that I have more than a name to worship. Thank You for all that You are to me. Amen.

GOOD-BYS

Saying good-by can be a sad experience. Recently I had a hard time saying good-by. I almost wished that I wouldn't have become so close to people I knew I'd have to leave; then it wouldn't hurt so much to say good-by. But looking back on the beauty of those friendships, I can better understand their purpose.

Life is a continual process of meeting people and leaving them, but no friendship is ever lost. Each friend becomes a part of me and I become a part of him or her, even though we aren't always together. Instead of complaining that I must leave friends, I should thank God for the time He gave us to be together. Then I can go on to make new friends and enjoy the immediate experiences of each new day.

Lord, when doubts fill my mind, when my heart is in turmoil, quiet me and give me renewed hope and cheer (Ps. 94:19 LB).

Thank You, Father, for the many beautiful friends You've brought into my life. Thank You for helping me see the beauty of friendship even when sometimes I have to say good-by. Amen.

STORMS OF LIFE

Storms, with thunder loud enough to make the windows rattle and lightning bright enough to light up the entire landscape, can be scary. Last summer we had a storm like that, and it felt like the end of the world was near: one more crack and the earth would split into pieces.

It made me think of the God who had control of all that chaos. He's much more powerful than the immense power of the storm which, in itself, was incomprehensible to me. Having God as my personal friend, I don't have to worry about big thunderstorms and all the other things in life that seem threatening. I have security in knowing that the storms in my life are nothing compared to the power Christ has to help me overcome them.

Though the earth shakes and all its people live in turmoil, yet its pillars are firm, for I have set them in place! (Ps. 75:3 LB).

Thank You, Lord, for being my personal friend even though I'm sometimes ungrateful and I don't deserve Your love. Thank You for Your great power to help me through the storms of life. Amen.

May 26

GOD'S IN CONTROL

Out of the darkness
Shall come dawn.
Out of our striving
Shall come peace.
Not by our power
But by the power of God.

I copied these words from a poster one of my friends had hanging on her door. Every time I read them, I'm reminded of the peace and rest which God gives. In a world that looks hopeless, I'm glad I'm in the hands of God, who has control of everything. By His power my efforts are rewarded.

Make every effort to keep the unity of the Spirit through the bond of peace (Eph. 4:3 NIV).

My God, I'm thankful that I don't have to struggle through darkness on my own power. Continue to be my strength. Amen.

BLOWING IN THE WIND

Last summer during a storm, an ugly, old, dead branch was blown out of the maple tree beside our house. It saved us the bother of cutting it off, so we were glad.

Strong winds in life can be of use too. Sometimes they do what nothing else can do — blow down dead branches which have detracted from the tree's appearance. Instead of trying to stop the wind from blowing, I should be aware of what needs to be blown out of my life and rejoice when it happens.

> **But because of his great love for us, God, who is rich in mercy, made us alive with Christ even when we were dead in transgressions — it is by grace you have been saved (Eph. 2:4,5 NIV).**

Keep the winds blowing in my life, Lord, to help clear away all that is hindering my appearance in Your sight. Amen.

WORK FOR GOD

Many people enjoy watching football games. While twenty-two tired people are working hard on the field, the stands are packed with spectators. They relate to the players but are uninvolved in the actual work of playing the game. The spectators may be in need of the exercise and they notice everything the players do wrong, but they leave the work to the few who are willing to play.

Life is much the same. A majority of the Christians are content to sit back and watch a few do the work. Unless I get into action and work for God, I can't expect to reap the benefits in the end.

He said to them, "Go into all the world and preach the good news to all creation" (Mark 16:15 NIV).

Motivate me, God, to start working for You and not be content to be a spectator, watching others do Your work alone. Amen.

PAIN AS WELL AS SUNSHINE

All sunshine makes a desert. If you've ever been on a hot, dry desert, you were probably thankful for an occasional cool breeze or rain. Similarly, in life the happy, bright days are preferred to the cloudy, rainy ones. But God, in His mercy, knows that too much sunshine would dry us up, so He provides all kinds of weather. I need to remember, when the clouds block out the sunshine, that every kind of weather is needed to produce the right climate for Christian growth.

Lord, grant us peace; for all we have and are has come from you (Isa. 26:12 LB).

Thank You, Lord, for clouds as well as sunshine. Let me be content in having You as my weather regulator. Amen.

FRUSTRATION

The definition of frustration is: "the blocking of the individual's progress toward a given goal or thwarting of the satisfaction of certain needs." The thing that strikes me in this is that frustration is caused when the *individual's* goals are blocked. Maybe I'm often frustrated needlessly because I make my own goals instead of asking first what God's goals are. He knows better than I what I can handle and how long it will take. Many times frustration can be eliminated when I'm willing to turn my goal-setting over to God.

A rebel's frustrations are heavier than sand and rocks (Prov. 27:3 LB).

O God, You know the goals I can meet. I pray that I will leave that job totally up to You. Amen.

THORNS OR ROSES?

Seeing the roses bloom at the beginning of summer reminds me of a poster that said, "You can complain because rosebushes have thorns, or rejoice because thorn bushes have roses."

The truth of that statement can be broadened to apply to much of life. When I'm willing to look long enough, something to be thankful for can usually be found. What looks bad at first glance may have value if it's seen from the right perspective.

You have done so much for me, O Lord. No wonder I am glad! (Ps. 92:4 LB).

Lord, teach me to look hard enough to find the good in things before I complain. Amen.

JUDAS

Little attention is given to Judas Iscariot except in relation to his betrayal of Jesus. Going beyond that fact, however, helped me see Judas in a different way.

Like the other eleven disciples, Judas was with Jesus, helping Him during His three years of ministry. He gave up his home and job to become a follower of Jesus. When Jesus said one of the Twelve would betray Him, none of them had any idea who it was, so Judas must not have done anything previously to make him seem guilty. After he betrayed Jesus, his grief was so deep that he couldn't face it. Yet even though Judas did some good for his Master, he is most remembered for the evil he committed.

> **When morning came, he called his disciples to him and chose twelve of them, whom he also designated apostles: Simon . . . and Judas Iscariot, who became a traitor (Luke 6:13,14,16 NIV).**

Help me, Father, not to prejudge other people even when the bad in them is more apparent. Help me to recognize that they have needs also. Amen.

MOTIVES AND ACTIONS

I remember the early spring days of my childhood when bright yellow dandelions covered our lawn and I picked huge handfuls to take proudly to mother. Even though dandelions wouldn't have been mother's favorite choice for a centerpiece, she always acted delighted as she helped me put all the short-stemmed weeds in a vase. It was my attitude of wanting to give her something that she appreciated, not necessarily the gift itself.

God is also more interested in the attitude in my heart when I do a good deed for Him than in what I do. It is important to live for Christ, but it doesn't amount to much unless my love and devotion to Him are the motives behind my actions.

And this is my prayer: that your love may abound more and more in knowledge and depth of insight, so that you may be able to discern what is best and may be pure and blameless until the day of Christ (Phil. 1:9,10 NIV).

Lord, guide my actions that they will grow only out of the right attitude in my heart. May my love and devotion to You be the most important motivating force in my life. Amen.

June 3

STAY IN TUNE

While taking a trip, we were listening to a radio station from Pittsburgh. The farther from Pittsburgh we traveled, however, the less distinct it became. Finally communication was lost completely. They were still broadcasting at the radio station, but we were too far away to hear it.

In my life, Jesus is the radio station I tune into. The closer I stay to Him, the better I hear His voice. He always remains at the same place. If He seems more distant at times, it's because I've moved. Jesus is constantly broadcasting. It's up to me to stay close enough to hear Him.

Neither height nor depth, nor anything else in all creation, will be able to separate us from the love of God that is in Christ Jesus our Lord (Rom. 8:39 NIV).

Thank You, Jesus, for broadcasting Your message continuously. Amen.

FINDING HAPPINESS

Happiness is a strange phenomenon. Sometimes it comes in abundance. Other times it's hidden so well I don't know if I'll ever find it again. I feel more and more that happiness can't be kept within, because only by reaching out can one find true happiness. The following way to happiness is of continual importance and I must remind myself of it anew every day:

> **H**elpfulness to others
> **A**lways kind
> **P**atience
> **P**raise for God
> **I**ntegrity within
> **N**ever envious
> **E**stablish friendly relationships
> **S**peak only what is good and pure
> **S**eek to love others more

Happy are those who long to be just and good, for they shall be completely satisfied (Matt. 5:6 LB).

Thank You for happy times, Lord. Teach me to seek happiness for others, forgetting my own desires. Amen.

FOOLISH QUESTIONS?

In a class where almost everyone was older and more experienced, I rarely asked questions. I was afraid the others would think my questions were foolish and insignificant. I either found the answers myself or asked someone after class.

When I think of God, with His infinite knowledge, many times greater than my wisest teacher, my problems and questions seem small. Nevertheless, another of His undescribable traits is that He cares about every problem I have, no matter how small. God will never make me feel foolish for any question I ask. Nothing is too great or too small for God.

> **For the Lord grants wisdom! His every word is a treasure of knowledge and understanding (Prov. 2:6 LB).**

Thank You, Teacher, for Your caring love which enables me to ask anything of You with the confidence that You won't think it's stupid. Amen.

June 6

SLOW DOWN

Done with my last exam of the school year, I kicked off my shoes and ran through the front lawn, enjoying the newly felt freedom. I was oblivious to all else, until . . . I stepped on the spot where a honeybee was working. It didn't waste any time letting me know it had been there first. That stopped me fast.

I heard God speaking to me through the sting of the bee. He seemed to be saying, "Enjoy your freedom, but be careful not to overstep your boundaries and hinder the freedom of another." It was a good reminder to me to remember others when the tendency is to think only of myself.

> **For I am not seeking my own good but the good of many, so that they may be saved (1 Cor. 10:33 NIV).**

Thank You, Father, for your small but unforgettable reminders to control my freedom if it interferes with someone else's. Amen.

WORK FOR GOD

Last year, when most of my friends were hunting summer jobs, I decided to stay home and help my parents. There was always plenty to do, but I felt lazy when friends asked me what I was doing for the summer. Working at home sounded like play compared to working in a factory or restaurant, even though it wasn't.

Then I saw a beautiful picture of Jesus that impressed me. As others went about their daily tasks, He sat by the side, talking to the children. It showed me that I, too, should be willing to do what I know is right without worrying about what others will think of me. If I'm pleasing God with my work, the opinion of others doesn't matter.

Jesus said, "Let the little children come to me, and do not hinder them, for the kingdom of heaven belongs to such as these" (Matt. 19:14 NIV).

Give me satisfaction, O God, in doing what's right when others don't see everything. Thank You for taking time out for the children, even though some of Your friends thought it was a waste of time. Amen.

WIN BY LOSING . . .

I asked God for strength, that I might achieve,
I was made weak, that I might learn humbly to obey . . .
I asked for health, that I might do greater things,
I was given infirmity, that I might do better things . . .
I asked for riches that I might be happy.
I was given poverty, that I might be wise . . .
I asked for power, that I might have the praise of men,

I was given weakness, that I might feel the need of
   God . . .
I asked for all things, that I might enjoy life,
I was given life, that I might enjoy all things . . .
I got nothing that I asked for — but everything I had
   hoped for,
Almost despite myself, my unspoken prayers were
   answered.
I am among all men most richly blessed.

— Anonymous

**I consider that our present sufferings are not worth
comparing with the glory that will be revealed in us
(Rom. 8:18 NIV).**

*Father, thank You for giving me what You know I need even if
I think I need something else. Amen.*

June 9

EXCITING CHANGES

Wherever God's people are united in prayer, exciting
changes are realized — changes in the life and spirit of the
church, but especially changes in people.

When God is allowed to enter and do His work in my life,
He does what needs doing, which sometimes means making radical changes. A life of prayer becomes evident to
each person it touches. Not only does prayer change individuals, but it also creates an image to others that makes
Christianity more attractive. People will more readily become a part of that which shows good fruit of what it
preaches.

**Ask and it will be given to you; seek and you will
find; knock and the door will be opened to you (Matt.
7:7 NIV).**

*Lord, make my times with You meaningful, and work Your
way in my life. May our relationship be one that non-Christians
will want to have also. Amen.*

EASTER IS EVERY DAY

Easter is a joyous time of celebrating the risen Savior. Every Easter Sunday I've gone to church and heard the Easter story through sermons, Sunday school lessons, and songs. At one particular Easter service, however, a poem was read that has stayed with me ever since. It said that Easter doesn't come only once a year, but it should be celebrated every day. The message of Christianity is that Christ rose from the dead for the sins of the world. Each day it is a new miracle.

He is not here; he has risen! (Luke 24:6 NIV).

Thank You, God, for the miracle of Your Son's rising from the dead. May I be reminded that Easter isn't only one day in the spring, but every day of my life. Amen.

NO BARRIER IN LANGUAGE

The science teacher took our class on a tour through the greenhouse. He had told us the day before about some of the plants and their names, but we couldn't picture their true beauty until we looked at them ourselves. We didn't need to know the names of the plants to enjoy them, but we had to see them.

In a time when many technical terms are used, it's easy to become confused with theological language. But whether or not I know the correct terminology, I can know the joy of Jesus' love and mercy. I only need to see big signs of His work.

For Christ did not send me to baptize, but to preach

the gospel — not with words of human wisdom, lest the cross of Christ be emptied of its power (1 Cor. 1:17 NIV).

Thank You, Jesus, that I don't need to know big words to be able to understand Your love. Be with me in sharing with others simply enough that they too can understand. Amen.

REINFORCING PRAISE

Jo Coudert writes, "Praise reinforces good traits, criticism bad traits. Criticism produces defensiveness; and no one acts well out of defensiveness: he is rattled, shaken, and hurt. Criticism causes the personality to shrink, to be diminished, and not only the personality of its target but of its deliverers as well."

The next time I'm tempted to criticize another's bad traits, I should stop and ask myself whether or not I'm part of the cause of those traits by my lack of praise.

Share with God's people who are in need (Rom. 12:13 NIV).

Teach me, Father, to praise rather than criticize. Show me ways I can be of help, not another hindrance. Amen.

EVERYONE IS A WITNESS

Many times it seems as though the responsibility of witnessing is given to the pastor. After all, that's his job. But, being the daughter of a pastor, I can testify to the fact that a pastor doesn't have more time than anyone else in the congregation. The pastor's job is to teach the people in his church, so they will be prepared to go out and share the gospel with their friends and neighbors. Spreading the gospel to the whole world is a bigger job than pastors can handle alone. Every follower of Christ is needed.

For we cannot help speaking about what we have seen and heard (Acts 4:20 NIV).

Lord, grant that I will never be satisfied to leave the job You've given me, of sharing Your love to others. Amen.

June 14

WITNESSING IS NECESSARY

Not only is witnessing a part of every Christian's responsibility, as was suggested yesterday, but it is also essential to the Christian life. Frank Laubach writes: "It has often been said that we cannot keep Jesus unless we give him away. . . . Spiritual life is like electricity. No current passes through unless the wire is connected at the sending end as well as at the receiving end." The congregation has not finished its task until every member is involved in witnessing.

Never be lacking in zeal, but keep your spiritual fervor, serving the Lord (Rom. 12:11 NIV).

I want to keep You, Jesus, by giving You away. May I always be a live wire for You. Amen.

June 15

GETTING ALONG WITH OTHERS

It has been said that if anyone wants to be happy and successful, he must learn to get along with others. One step toward this is to be interested in others. More friends can be won in a month by my being interested in them than in ten years by trying to get them interested in me.

Being interested in others may mean putting my own interests aside to become involved in theirs. It may mean doing my job and forgetting about receiving credit for it. It may also mean meeting criticism with good will and love. Whatever the means, showing interest in others will produce rich blessings.

Nobody should seek his own good, but the good of others (1 Cor. 10:24 NIV).

Teach me, O Lord, to forget myself in the interest of others. Amen.

June 16

GETTING ALONG WITH MYSELF

Another guide to a happy and successful life is the ability to get along with oneself. Conflicts with others usually stem from conflicts within ourselves. When children become fussy and irritable, it's usually a sign that it's their bedtime. The same is true with adults. When I am easily bothered by others, it's a sign that I should look inside myself for the reason. When I settle my own inner disturbances, others tend to disturb me less.

Be joyful in hope, patient in affliction, faithful in prayer (Rom. 12:12 NIV).

When I become irritated, Lord, remind me to look for the cause within myself — not to blame others. Amen.

June 17

FAITH — NOT FEELING

"But I don't *feel* like a Christian." Have you ever said that? I've heard similar statements from friends and have felt that way myself. It's really quite a normal feeling.

When I don't feel like a Christian these are the best times to form and strengthen my faith. I must keep going on the knowledge of life in Christ, and the good feelings will return. God is always faithful, waiting for my faith to return. As Joe Bayly said, "Don't forget in the darkness what you've learned in the light."

If we are faithless, he will remain faithful, for he cannot disown himself (2 Tim. 2:13 NIV).

Thank You, Father, that I can know by faith that I am Your child, even if the feelings aren't always present. Amen.

June 18

MOUNTAIN CLIMBING

Life is like a mountain, and each person must climb his own. Each mountain has many hidden places to go through, rough spots, and dips. The end is not visible, but everyone does have an end.

Many differences exist between these mountains, however. Some are steeper than others. Some have more rough places and bigger dips. Some climbers take more time to see the beauty of their mountain and enjoy it instead of merely striving to reach the top.

The biggest difference is having Jesus as the Guide up the mountain. When I'm in a dip and Jesus seems to be gone, I know He's only over the next ridge calling me; and if I keep going, He will be waiting for me. He will never let me slip back as long as I keep my eyes on Him. Jesus doesn't make the mountain less steep, but He makes the climb worthwhile.

And we know that in all things God works for the good of those who love him, who have been called according to his purpose (Rom. 8:28 NIV).

Thank You, Jesus, for being my constant Guide up life's mountain. Help me always to keep my eyes fixed on You. Amen.

BEGIN IN THE SOUL

A Chinese proverb says:

> If there is right in the soul,
> There will be beauty in the person;
> If there is beauty in the person,
> There will be harmony in the home;
> If there is harmony in the home,
> There will be order in the nation;
> If there is order in the nation,
> There will be peace in the world.

Too many times I look at things that seem impossible to change. I should, instead, begin with myself and see if everything is as it should be. Only then can I try to change other things.

Why do you look at the speck of sawdust in your brother's eye and pay no attention to the plank in your own eye? (Luke 6:41 NIV).

Lord, teach me to set goals that I can handle before trying to change the whole world. Amen.

LEARN TO SAY NO

"Why did I let myself get into this? Why didn't I just tell them I couldn't do it?" Does that sound familiar? Many times I find myself asking these questions, but by then it's too late.

I once heard Arthur McPhee, a Mennonite pastor, speak on the subject of learning to say no. He said, "Your yeses don't mean much until you've learned to say no." I suddenly realized that it isn't the number of things I say yes to that's important, but what I say no to.

For each man should carry his own load (Gal. 6:5 NIV).

Lord, guide me in knowing when to say yes and when to say no. Amen.

June 21

LIFE'S GREATEST AIM

If asked what my greatest aim in life is, I might answer with a big dream, like to bring peace to the entire world. That goal would be nice, but I can't possibly accomplish it alone. In 1 Corinthians, Paul gives us a command from the Lord: love is to be our greatest aim. That sounds easy enough! I love everyone already.

But then He explains what His love means, and when I think of specific people it gets harder and harder to say I love them. "Love is very patient and kind, never jealous or envious." Wow! It's tough not to wish I could live in a house like the neighbors have, or dress like my friend. "Never haughty or selfish or rude." I guess I wasn't being very loving yesterday when my sister had to wash the dishes alone because I was reading a good book. "It is not irritable or touchy." But, Lord, how can I love that guy who always makes me feel stupid in English class?

I can't love — alone. By my own power, I can't love everyone, but through Christ, everything is possible. He can help me love people who seemed unlovable before.

And now these three remain: faith, hope and love. But the greatest of these is love (1 Cor. 13:13 NIV).

Christ, help me to make love my greatest aim in life. Teach me

how it's possible to really love everyone because You made them
and You love them. Amen.

BY GOD'S WISDOM

The more I learn, the more there seems yet to learn. Looking at a small flower under a microscope, I realize how intricate and amazing each tiny part of God's creation is. Listening to the many different bird calls makes me think of how much God cares, that He gave each bird its own identity. With the entrance of each baby into the world, a new miracle takes place. Hearing scholars answer the same questions with many different answers reminds me that only God knows everything. It makes me wonder how often God looks at the foolishness of man's wisdom and wonders why man thinks he has the answers.

> **If you want favor with both God and man, and a reputation for good judgment and common sense, then trust the Lord completely; don't ever trust yourself (Prov. 3:4,5 LB).**

Your wisdom is vast, Father. Grant that I will never think I know more than You've helped me to understand. Amen.

June 23

LIFE IS FOR LIVING

The butterflies fluttered wildly in my stomach as the time came closer to give my report in front of the class. This kind of stress is common in many situations. Sometimes stress is considered bad, something to be avoided.

But according to Hans Selye, author of *Stress Without*

Distress, stress is a fact of life. "Since stress is associated with all types of activity," he explains, "we could avoid most of it only by never doing anything. Who would enjoy a life of no runs, no hits, no errors?"

God wants me to enjoy living without worrying about the stress that might come. That would merely add more stress.

If God is for us, who can be against us? (Rom. 8:31 NIV).

God, help me not to let the threat of stress hinder me from enjoying life, but to trust You to care for me through each trial. Amen.

June 24

WHERE IS GOD?

As I rode through the city I wondered where God was. All I saw were tall, dark buildings crowded together, with masses of people going in and out of them. Many different noises could be heard: sirens, yelling, screeching brakes. Everyone seemed to be involved in his own world, oblivious to those around him.

Then we passed an old building with a beautiful pink flower growing in front of it. It was as if God was calling out, "I'm here too." Then I knew that He had been there all the time. I just hadn't looked hard enough for Him. God is wherever I become aware of Him.

They asked each other, "Were not our hearts burning within us while he talked with us on the road and opened the Scriptures to us?" (Luke 24:32 NIV).

Thank You, God, for Your presence wherever I look for You. Help me as I search for You when You aren't as easy to see. Amen.

OPEN TO THE SPIRIT

The sense of hearing is funny sometimes. People can train themselves not to hear certain things. My younger brother became good at not hearing mother say it was time to do his homework. I can train myself not to hear my alarm clock if I know someone else will hear it and waken me later. The mind can become so accustomed to a sound that it no longer makes an impact.

My soul can become so accustomed to the Holy Spirit's call that after awhile it is quite deaf. The longer I block Him out of my life, the farther away He will seem. The Holy Spirit speaks only to those who are listening and ready to obey.

Do not put out the Spirit's fire (1 Thess. 5:19 NIV).

Father, thank You for Your gift of the Holy Spirit. I pray that I will always be listening for His guidance in my life. Amen.

FOLLOW ME

I remember the first meeting I attended where an invitation was given for all who wanted to follow Jesus to go forward. I felt Jesus was calling me — my heart pounded wildly, but I was too afraid to go. I wanted more time to think about it and take into consideration all that would be involved.

Just recently, as I was reading in the Gospels how Jesus called His twelve disciples, a new thought struck me. When Jesus said, "Follow me," the Scriptures say they dropped whatever they were doing and followed Him. It doesn't tell us anything about the thoughts and doubts that might have gone through the disciples' heads. Their immediate responses to Jesus' call indicate no hesitancy.

That's how my life should be too. When I hear Christ's call, I must answer it without trying to rationalize every move. The twelve disciples are good examples of what it means to live in immediate obedience to Jesus.

> **As he was walking up the beach he saw Levi, the son of Alphaeus, sitting at his tax collection booth. "Come with me," Jesus told him. "Come be my disciple." And Levi jumped to his feet and went along (Mark 2:14 LB).**

Master, let me walk with You; not thinking everything over reasonably, but with the faith that Your calling is enough. Amen.

June 27

LOOK FOR THE OPEN DOOR

Alexander Graham Bell said, "When one door closes, another opens; but we often look so long and so regretfully upon the closed door that we do not see the one which has opened for us." As an inventor, he probably had to learn to keep looking for new things when one thing didn't work.

In much the same way, Christ opens and shuts doors for His children. Sometimes shut doors are painful, and it's difficult to see the doors that are opening right away. But if we search diligently, doors will open. God doesn't shut doors unless He has a better one to open.

> **In him the whole building is joined together and rises to become a holy temple in the Lord (Eph. 2:21 NIV).**

Thank You, Jesus, for controlling the doors in my life. Guide me in knowing which are opened and closed to me. Amen.

THE IMPORTANCE OF SMALL THINGS

A badly needed rain blessed our garden for several hours, helping the vegetables like nothing else could have. When Hurricane Agnes swept through the country, doing immeasurable damage, it was broadcast around the world. These examples showed me that the most effective things are not measured by how well they're publicized. Small things can be of greater importance than larger things. Like the summer rain, I need to do things to be helpful rather than to gain recognition. God sees all that I do, and my efforts should be to please Him, not other people.

Therefore, whoever humbles himself like this child is the greatest in the kingdom of heaven (Matt. 18:4 NIV).

Teach me, Father, to humble myself to do the necessary small jobs and be satisfied with no recognition from men. Amen.

WHO ARE YOU KIDDING?

When a person refuses to go to church because it's too hot, then goes to the beach instead, who is he kidding? When a person doesn't have enough money to tithe but lives in a nice home, has plenty to eat and wear, and drives a nice car, who is he kidding? When a person can't stay awake during a twenty-minute sermon, yet stays up to watch the late show, who is he kidding? When a person stays away from church because there are too many people, but goes to crowded football games, who is he kidding? When a person does whatever he wants to do all week, then is too tired to go to church on Sunday, who is he kidding? Not God!

"It is mine to avenge, I will repay," says the Lord (Rom. 12:19 NIV).

O God, grant that I never try to fool You by making silly excuses for not doing what I know is right. Amen.

June 30

ENRICHING COMPLIMENTS

Everyone has seen what a compliment can do for a person. Mark Twain once said, "I can live for two months on a good compliment." Not only is the recipient of the compliment being blessed, but also the person giving it. What is said aloud is remembered better and believed longer. Good feelings toward another enrich both sides of the relationship. As Oscar Wilde put it, "It is a great mistake for men to give up paying compliments, for when they give up saying what is charming, they give up thinking what is charming."

Do not let any unwholesome talk come out of your mouths, but only what is helpful for building others up according to their needs, that it may benefit those who listen (Eph. 4:29 NIV).

Thank You, Father, for the many times I've been brought happiness by either receiving a compliment or by giving a compliment. Amen.

BELIEVE IN GOD

At first, "believing" and "believing in" may seem to represent the same idea, but they are really two different concepts. Believing is done in the mind, whereas believing in something calls for action. A step of faith is needed to work for the cause and become completely involved.

Jesus calls His followers not only to believe, but also to believe in Him. His calling requires knowledge and the action to carry out that knowledge successfully.

> **For God so loved the world that he gave his one and only Son, that whoever believes in him shall . . . have everlasting life (John 3:16 NIV).**

I want to be aware of what it involves to believe in You, Jesus. May I never be satisfied to only believe You. Amen.

A STURDY FOUNDATION

One of my favorite things to do at the beach is to build sand castles. It's fun to see who can build the biggest, sturdiest, and fanciest castle. Each time, however, when we return the next day, the tide has washed them away.

A fishing pier along the same shore has continued to stand. Its foundation is deep and sturdy enough to give it strength against the tides.

We had done the best job possible with sand, but it wasn't good enough. Neither can I build a good enough protection against the tides of life without Jesus giving me a deep and sturdy foundation.

> **But everyone who hears these words of mine and**

does not put them into practice is like a foolish man who built his house on sand (Matt. 7:26 NIV).

I don't need to be washed around like sand on the beach with You, Jesus. Thank You for being my Foundation to build on. Amen.

BLESSINGS OF REST FROM WORK

I remember a spring when everything seemed to be off to a good start. The fruit trees were full of blossoms and the gardens were green with early crops. Then came a killing frost, putting an end to their productivity for another year.

I had a similar experience once. I was working hard at several tasks at once, trying frantically to get everything done. Then I became sick and was forced to stay in bed. I soon found out I wasn't essential for the work after all. Life kept going without me and things were done even when I didn't help. I was shown that it doesn't pay to work so hard that I'm soon worn out. Then I'm of no use at all.

O Lord, you have freed me from my bonds and I will serve you forever (Ps. 116:16 LB).

Thank You, Lord, for showing me when I need to slow down. I give You control of my life to keep working in me. Amen.

CELEBRATE!

On the evening of July 4, my brothers, sister, and I went out in the yard to watch the fireworks, which were clearly visible from a mile away. They were showy displays with many beautiful colors spurting out in all directions.

This incident made me think about my Christian life. I wondered if I was making visible the joy and beauty of my life with Christ, not only to those who are close to me, but also to those farther away.

If fireworks go all out to celebrate the freedom of our country, how much more should I celebrate the freedom I experience through Christ!

Let your light shine before men, that they may see your good deeds and praise your Father in heaven (Matt. 5:16 NIV).

Forgive me, Jesus, when I have not shown the joy You give me, so that others will know how wonderful You are. Guide me as I seek to spread Your love. Amen.

July 5

CHRIST AS THE FLASHLIGHT

A group of friends and I decided to go camping in the woods one night. Since it was dark when we arrived and there were no lights anywhere around, we used flashlights. By their light it was easy to find our way in the darkness.

Sometimes, the world seems dark and scary. I'm not sure what lies ahead. But I can move forward with confidence as Christ lights my path. What looks dark and formidable at first is made much less scary when I know Jesus is with me.

Your words are a flashlight to light the path ahead of me, and keep me from stumbling (Ps. 119:105 LB).

Lord, thank You for lighting my path through dark times. Teach me to stay on the path and keep my eyes on You. Amen.

LAUGH WITH OTHERS

Telling my younger brother something funny is really enjoyable. He's already laughing so hard when I'm only half done that I don't need to finish the story. He has a real talent to laugh with others, which makes him fun to be with.

Everyone needs someone with whom to share joys as well as sorrows. Sometimes being happy with another is the harder of the two, but it is just as important. If a brother or sister is happy when I'm not, I must learn to forget myself and rejoice with him or her.

Rejoice with those who rejoice (Rom. 12:15 NIV).

Thank You, Father, for the ability to laugh and share happiness with others. Thank You also for all those who share in my happiness. Amen.

STAND UP FOR JESUS

"Stand up, stand up for Jesus" — those are words from a hymn written by George Duffield, inspired by a dying minister. The minister had been driven out of his church for speaking out against slavery. When Duffield asked him on his deathbed, if he had any words for his people, he said, "Yes, tell them to stand up for Jesus."

Too many times I fail to stand up for Jesus. I'm content to keep my convictions to myself and not let others know who's the Master of my life. I must remember that if I speak boldly about Jesus, it will encourage others to stand up for Him and He will receive the glory.

Paul and Barnabas spent considerable time there, speaking boldly for the Lord, who confirmed the message of his grace by enabling them to do miraculous signs and wonders (Acts 14:3 NIV).

O Master of my life, help me to let others know of You and not to be content to hide Your presence in me. Amen.

ADMIT IT

Some of the most difficult words to say to someone and really mean them are, "I'm sorry. It's my fault. Will you forgive me?" Yet they're essential to good relationships.

Selfishness tries to rationalize wrong actions and blame another. The longer I wait to confess a wrong, the harder it becomes. The line that says, "Love means never needing to say you're sorry," is all wrong according to Jesus. He loves me more than I can imagine, yet I must confess my sins to Him so He can forgive them. Peace can only come through admitting when I'm wrong.

If we confess our sins, he is faithful and just and will forgive us our sins and purify us from all unrighteousness (1 John 1:9 NIV).

Teach me, Father, that real love says "I'm sorry" many times. Thank You for Your unlimited forgiveness. Amen.

A NEW APPEARANCE

I watched the changes as I rubbed the wax on the car, making the once-dull finish so shiny I could see myself in it. I was amazed at the difference cleaning, waxing, and polishing had made.

Christ's redeeming power can make a lot of difference in my life too. By a daily renewal of my relationship with Him, I can retain the sparkle and appeal of faith and continue in His work. When I'm willing to submit my life for God to clean up and polish, an amazing transformation can take place.

Sprinkle me with the cleansing blood and I shall be clean again. Wash me and I shall be whiter than snow (Ps. 51:7 LB).

Take my life, O God, and clean it with Your perfection. Amen.

July 10

WORK FOR THE LORD

Last summer I worked at a monotonous job. I stuffed envelopes in a factory. Time usually went slowly, so to pass the hours, we had races to see who could stuff the fastest, made up all kinds of games, listened to the radio, sang, and talked about every imaginable subject.

Being of the opinion that everything a Christian does should be for God's glory, I tried to think of what glory He was receiving. I found that even in a monotonous summer job, some good can be found. Working just as hard and fast when the boss isn't watching is one sign of working for a higher authority. Another sign is staying cheerful through the long hours.

Working for God is more rewarding than just receiving a pay check. The pay check only comes every other week, but God's rewards come after each day of good work.

Work hard and cheerfully at all you do, just as though you were working for the Lord and not merely for your masters, remembering that it is the Lord Christ who is going to pay you (Col. 3:23,24 LB).

I pray, Lord, that I will always do my best for You at work, even if no one is watching and no matter how hard the job is. Amen.

GOD GIVES ROAD SIGNS

A friend and I decided to go shopping in a distant town, where neither of us had been before. We started out not knowing the way, but confident that with the help of the road signs, we shouldn't have any trouble finding our destination.

That kind of experience doesn't sound scary, but it seems when God calls me to leave what I know and travel into the unknown, I'm afraid. I forget that He too promises to give me road signs along the way to direct me to where He's leading. When life's road becomes puzzling and intricate, it's comforting to know I'm not following my own directions.

For this great God is our God forever and ever. He will be our guide until we die (Ps. 48:14 LB).

Thank You, Father, for guidance down the road You've called me to travel. May I always remember to watch for Your road signs. Amen.

WHEN THE OTHER FELLOW . . .

When the other fellow acts that way, he's ugly . . .
When you do it, it's nerves.
When he's set in his ways, he's obstinate . . .
When you are, it's just firmness.
When he doesn't like your friends, he's prejudiced . . .
When you don't like his, you are simply showing good
    judgment of human nature.
When he tries to be accommodating, he's polishing the
    apple . . .

When you do it, you're using tact.
When he takes time to do things, he is dead slow . . .
When you take ages, you are deliberate.
When he picks flaws, he's cranky . . .
When you do, you're discriminating.

These words by an anonymous writer capture the tendency of self-justification found in each of us if we aren't careful.

> **For in the same way you judge others, you will be judged, and with the measure you use, it will be measured to you (Matt. 7:2 NIV).**

Lord, guide me today and every day to see another's actions as I would my own. Amen.

July 13

GOOD ATMOSPHERE

When man first landed on the moon, many craters were discovered on its surface, most of which were caused by meteors. Meteors are not burned up before impact because the moon has no atmosphere. Scientists estimate that over two hundred million meteors enter the earth's atmosphere each day, but most of them are burned up before they reach the earth.

The heart also must have an atmosphere to protect it from the threatening meteors of life. It's a defense against the pressures and words thrown at me each day. With Christ in my heart, many situations can be burned down to a size I can handle.

> **Keep your heart with all vigilance; for from it flows the springs of life (Prov. 4:23 RSV).**

The atmosphere You give my heart, Lord, will help keep evil from it. Thank You for Your protection. Amen.

INFECTIONS

Through modern medicine, it's now possible to be inoculated against many kinds of diseases and infections. Other kinds of infections are important to guard against also, even though no medical protection is available.

It is impossible to be isolated in life from all temptation and evil, but much of it can be avoided. As a Christian, I also have an inoculation against infection in my spiritual life — Jesus. He gives me help in seeking the good things in life, and with both of us working together, infection can be kept away.

How can a young man stay pure? By reading your Word and following its rules (Ps. 119:9 LB).

Thank You, Jesus, for being my protection against the infections to my spiritual well-being in this life. Help me overcome the temptations and pressures of my society and live totally for You. Amen.

IT'S HARD TO IMAGINE

As I stood on the beach watching the waves pound against the shore, I marveled once again at the power of the ocean. Man has learned to control many things, but nothing on earth can prevent the tide or stop the waves.

For me the ocean symbolizes God. It's hard to imagine a God who made the powerful ocean, which in itself is beyond my perception. It's also hard to imagine why I wouldn't want to give my life to such a powerful God every day.

**You alone are my God; my times are in your hands
(Ps. 31:15 LB).**

*Thank You, mighty God, for Your strength that watches over
me all the time. Continue to make Your presence known. Amen.*

GIVING ACCOUNT

As a child, when I did something wrong, I tried to blame
it on someone else. Sometimes it worked; sometimes it
didn't. Today it's still hard for me to take responsibility for
my mistakes.

As far back as Cain and Abel, man has provided exam-
ples of that human trait of disclaiming responsibility.
When God asked Cain where Abel was, Cain responded,
"Am I my brother's keeper?"

Occasionally it's possible to pass the responsibility off on
someone else, but we can never fool God. Each person is
held accountable in the Book of Life for what he does.

**And each person was judged according to what he
had done (Rev. 20:13 NIV).**

*Teach me to face up to my own actions, O God. Get rid of that
evil in me that I don't want to recognize. Amen.*

HANDLING GOD'S MONEY

Money is a test of character and a surprising number of
verses in the Scriptures speak to the subject. One person
claims that in the synoptic Gospels, one verse of every six
refers to money, either directly or indirectly. Money is
involved in sixteen of the Lord's thirty-three parables.

J. Oswald Sanders in his book *A Spiritual Clinic* states, "There is often a very definite connection between weakness in the spiritual life and failure in the stewardship of money." It is easy to make excuses for not giving to God, but no excuse is good enough.

Remembering the words of the Lord Jesus: "It is more blessed to give than to receive" (Acts 20:35 NIV).

Your blessings are bountiful, Lord, and everything I have is from You. Help me to be generous with what You've given me. Amen.

July 18

JESUS AT MEALTIME

Sometimes I think of a congregation as a large group of people gathered together in a church building for a specific service. But Jesus said that if as few as two or three are congregated in His name, He will be with them.

When the two disciples, on their way to Emmaus after Jesus' death, walked with Jesus, they didn't recognize Him until He sat down to eat with them.

Jesus is the guest at each meal today, too, when we ask His blessing on our food. Even though He's not visible as He was to those disciples, we can be assured of His presence, making mealtimes a worshipful experience.

When he was at the table with them, he took bread, gave thanks, broke it and began to give it to them (Luke 24:30 NIV).

Thank You, Jesus, for being my personal companion and not just revealing Your presence when many people are gathered together in Your name. Amen.

THE PERFECT ONE

Luke records the story of Jesus telling Simon Peter to let down his net after a night of being unable to catch any fish. Peter was astounded by the miraculous results of the huge catch. Realizing Jesus' greatness, Peter recognized the reality of his own sins, and he told Him to go away.

It disturbs me, too, when I see my life beside the life of Jesus, the Perfect One. Escape is impossible, and Jesus doesn't want me to leave Him. He wants me to learn from Him. Only by staying beside Him through my failures can I learn from His perfection.

When Simon Peter saw this, he fell at Jesus' knees and said, "Go away from me, Lord; I am a sinful man!" (Luke 5:8 NIV).

Dear Jesus, thank You for Your perfection and Your compassion for me, a sinner. Draw me closer to You that I might learn from You. Amen.

TO THE END OF THE AGE

When I measure myself by God's divine standard, I am quickly put to shame by my shortcomings. But instead of feeling defeated, it should urge me to improve. By having God as my example, I can always ask myself what His will is in any situation. I can improve by seeing myself through His eyes.

God doesn't want me to be so overcome by His greatness that I give up. He promised to be with me to the end of time, to help me to continually become more Christlike.

Following Him leads to a deep appreciation that He will never leave me.

And surely I will be with you always, to the very end of the age (Matt. 28:20 NIV).

Father, help me to look to Your example without becoming discouraged. Thank You for Your divine guidance. Amen.

July 21

GOD'S WORD BOOMERANGS

My brother received a boomerang as a gift one year. When he threw it into the air, it circled and came back to him. Although he just had fun with it, the real purpose of a boomerang is to kill birds.

God's Word is like a boomerang. It returns to Him only after it has accomplished its purpose. God gives His Word to His followers and trusts them to send it out. He promises to give His Word to anyone who opens his mouth for His sake. I don't need to be afraid when I speak for God. I can be sure His words won't return to Him empty, but I can be an instrument in helping to accomplish His purpose.

So shall my word be that goes forth from my mouth; it shall not return to me empty, but it shall accomplish that which I purpose, and prosper in the thing for which I sent it (Isa. 55:11 RSV).

Lord God, let me be a boomerang for You in sending forth Your Word. Thank You for the words You give me to say. Amen.

July 22

GOING DIRECTLY TO GOD

Shopping in a new grocery store can be frustrating the first few times. Items are hard to find until their location is learned.

I had such an experience when I was asked to get something from a store where I had never been before. I looked a long time without success. I didn't want to ask a clerk because I thought I could soon find it by myself. I finally broke down, however, and asked for help. He showed me exactly where it was.

Life can be like that too. I try to do something on my own until I can't go any more. Then I go crying to God for help. It would be easier if I'd go to God right away without first relying on my own knowledge.

Let us then approach the throne of grace with confidence, so that we may receive mercy and find grace to help us in our time of need (Heb. 4:16 NIV).

Heavenly Father, forgive me for the times I thought I could handle a situation alone. Thank You for helping me. Amen.

July 23

LEARNING FROM THE BIRDS

Within nature there are many lessons waiting to be discovered. I haven't begun to learn all of them, but the birds taught me one.

While bird-watching, I listened to the songs of the birds. Each bird sounded different. Then I noticed that they were all singing at once — not just the ones who could sing best, nor the ones with the most beautiful feathers. Each was singing his best, and it didn't seem to bother him a bit if another bird was singing something different.

I have learned from the birds that I need to think less of how my song or what I wear compares to another person's. I should sing the song God has given me as well as I can and be satisfied with that.

And the birds nest beside the streams and sing among the branches of the trees (Ps. 104:12 LB).

Great Creator, thank You for the song You've given me to sing. Give me, also, a joy in singing it that refuses to compare it to another. Amen.

LIGHT OUT OF DARKNESS

Our family was with a group of tourists one summer, touring a huge cave below the Virginia mountains. The cave was lighted occasionally by electric lights, so we could see the path through what would have otherwise been dark.

Then our guide announced that he would turn off the lights so we could feel what complete darkness was really like. It could have been scary if I hadn't kept in mind that the guide had the power to make it light again.

When circumstances in life change suddenly and everything looks dark, it's scary. Fear can be banished, however, by remembering that God has the power to bring light out of darkness. When I put my faith in Him, I don't need to walk in the dark.

When darkness overtakes him, light will come bursting in (Ps. 112:4 LB).

God, O Light of my path, thank You for providing a way out of the darkness that sometimes surrounds me. Amen.

THE GREATEST INVITATION

I read the invitation again. It would be exciting to go to my friend's wedding. Probably a lot of other old friends would be there too, and I looked forward to seeing them again.

As I hurried to write my acceptance of the invitation, I remembered another invitation I had accepted many months before. It was from Jesus, who said, "Come unto me." I accepted His invitation too and it has made the biggest difference in my life.

I knew my friend's wedding would be happy. But it couldn't begin to be compared to the greatest wedding of all — when Christ comes for His church. At that wedding there will be no parting.

> **The Spirit and the bride say, "Come!" And let him who hears say, "Come!" . . . Whoever wishes, let him take the free gift of the water of life (Rev. 22:17 NIV).**

Thank You, Father, for Your glorious invitation. May I always be worthy of being Your guest. Amen.

THE COST OF WORSHIP

The Bible tells of many times when people traveled far for the sake of Jesus. The Magi traveled for months to see Him when He was born. People went out to the desert from Jerusalem, Judea, and the Jordan region to hear John the Baptist preach about His coming. During Jesus' ministry, large crowds followed Him wherever He went.

How different the story is today. Some have a hard time getting out of bed once a week to go to church. People in Jesus' day would have a hard time understanding why people with so many modern conveniences, easy travel and transportation, and more leisure time than they ever knew, don't have time to go and hear God's Word. Are we taking too much for granted?

Large crowds from Galilee, the Decapolis, Jerusalem, Judea, and the region across the Jordan followed him (Matt. 4:25 NIV).

Forgive me, Father, for the many times I have taken Your Word for granted. Help me to see the foolishness of my excuses to not worship You. Amen.

FORGIVENESS

"Forgive." I've found that to be one of the most difficult commandments for me to keep. It's not so hard to say I forgive someone, but to completely forget it can be almost impossible.

Sometimes it doesn't seem fair that I have to forgive people. Then I think of God's forgiveness and His never-ending love. It wasn't fair that His Son, who never sinned, had to die a horrible death on the cross for my sins — but He did.

By our earthly laws, it doesn't seem right that if I do something wrong, I can have complete forgiveness without paying the consequences, but I can. Even when I knowingly turn my back on God, He readily takes me back into His loving arms when I want to come. He keeps no records of sins forgiven.

For if you forgive men when they sin against you, your heavenly Father will also forgive you. But if you do not forgive men their sins, your Father will not forgive your sins (Matt. 6:14,15 NIV).

Lord, teach me complete forgiveness. When I have a difficult time forgiving others, remind me of the many times You've graciously forgiven me, and help me to be more Christlike. Amen.

BLOSSOM

The rosebud on the table at the front of the church signified that a baby had been born to one of the families in our congregation. The petals were tightly closed, showing only the beauty of the outer few. Much of the beauty remained inside, hidden until the rose was given time to mature and unfold.

Babies and young Christians are much the same as the rosebud. At first, gifts and talents are undeveloped and can't be seen. But when the bud of faith is nourished by the Word of God and His Spirit, it blossoms out to become a full flower in Christ's work.

They are like trees along a river bank bearing luscious fruit each season without fail. Their leaves shall never wither, and all they do shall prosper (Ps. 1:3 LB).

Gracious Father, bless me with Your gifts that I may become beautiful in Spirit and fruitful for Your service. Amen.

SPIRITUAL STRENGTH

Sometimes it's hard to get children interested in eating. They don't seem to realize that they need food to give them strength and help them grow. Even if they're hungry, they don't want to take time to eat.

Often Christians act like children. Just as food is needed for physical strength, spiritual strength is found by prayer and reading God's Word. Even when I'm hungry and weak spiritually, I sometimes forget the nourishment I really need. Growth doesn't happen automatically. It takes a lot of time and effort. Only when I am fortified with prayer and

God's Word do I have the power to let God work through me.

Search for him and for his strength, and keep on searching! (Ps. 105:4 LB).

O Lord, I ask that the desire for spiritual nourishment will become as natural as the desire for food for physical strength. May I always be aware of my need for You. Amen.

KING OF KINGS

In Handel's oratorio *Messiah* there is a moment which seems to have everyone under its enchantment — when the "Hallelujah Chorus" majestically proclaims, "King of Kings and Lord of Lords . . . forever and ever. Hallelujah!"

No one can yet see everything God is King and Lord over, but we have seen Him crowned with honor and glory. We know that nothing can defeat Him. He rose from the grave and is now reigning as King over the entire world. With God as the Lord of the universe and my personal Lord as well, I have nothing to fear from the kings and rulers of this world.

The kingdom of the world has become the kingdom of our Lord and of his Christ, and he will reign for ever and ever (Rev. 11:15 NIV).

Lord and King, thank You for ruling my life so I don't need to be concerned about the rulers and kings of this world. Amen.

LOVE INTO MATURITY

My younger brother was delighted when he was given a lively puppy for his birthday. During the weeks that followed, our family learned that having a puppy meant scratches, bites, a messed-up house, ruined clothing, and sometimes a rude awakening in the morning. Through all the irritating things the hyperactive puppy did, my brother continued to love and care for him. Because of my brother's patience, the dog eventually calmed down and everyone enjoyed him.

In the Christian family, some members may require extra patience in their growth. I need to feel the responsibility to stick by a brother or sister with love, as my own brother loved his dog into maturity.

Show mercy and kindness and tender compassion every man to his brother (Zech. 7:9 *Amplified***).**

Give me patience, Lord, to love people who seem hard to love at first. Help me to accept them as my brothers and sisters in Your family. Amen.

PULLING WEEDS

When we arrived home from vacation, weeds had taken over our garden. It looked like a hopeless mess; perhaps the best thing to do would be to give it up. Instead, we doubled our efforts to get rid of the weeds so the vegetables could grow freely again.

Life can easily become like a weedy garden. After the seeds are planted, the weeds of the world come up around the good plants. If the weeds aren't pulled, they will choke out the plants. When I grow discouraged by all the evil I see, I must double my efforts to bring the good into sight again.

Let us not become weary in doing good, for at the proper time we will reap a harvest if we do not give up (Gal. 6:9 NIV).

Father, let me not grow weary of keeping the weeds out of my life. Thank You for the strength and courage You give to work at it. Amen.

LOVE IS SHARING

Recently I received a letter from a close friend in which she was asking herself some questions that made me think too. If I claim that Christ means more to me than anything else, how can I be slow to share Him with others? How can I know someone long without telling him or her what is most important to me? How can I really love a person and yet hold back that which can add unlimited beauty to his or her life?

The answer is that I can't. To love as Christ loves means

sharing His love. Only selfishness can cause me to with-hold the most beautiful part of my life — Jesus Christ.

He has given me a new song to sing, of praises to our God (Ps. 40:3 LB).

Lord Jesus, thank You for the song You've put in my heart to sing for You. Give me courage to sing it out for You in love. Amen.

RUINED BY NEGLECT

Wanting to ride bikes one afternoon, I went to the garage to find the bike I had ridden when I was younger. I was disappointed to see rust and dust covering the frame, tires needing air, and crooked handlebars.

Neglect can ruin my life with Christ too. If I don't con-tinue to use what I know and mature in my faith, I will become as useless as the bicycle that was stored away without being ridden or cared for. I can keep my witness strong by continuing to use the Spirit's fruit in me.

But whoever lives by the truth comes into the light, so that it may be seen plainly that what he has done has been done through God (John 3:21 NIV).

Forgive me, Father, for times when I've neglected putting Your Word into practice. Thank You for Your reminder to keep growing. Amen.

CELEBRATE CHRISTMAS IN AUGUST

Summer is the easiest time of the year to become self-centered, but there's really no excuse for it. Being out of school provides more time to give to others.

Christmas is perhaps the busiest time of the year, but people usually find time to sing at nursing homes, visit friends, give gifts, and do many other special things. I should find time to practice the Christmas spirit throughout the entire year. I will probably find it more rewarding to be kind to people when they aren't expecting it!

And God is able to make all grace abound to you, so that in all things at all times, having all that you need, you will abound in every good work (2 Cor. 9:8 NIV).

Lord, give me the Christmas spirit in August and in every other month of the year. Show me ways to portray Your love all year long. Amen.

August 5

A NEW CREATION

My grandfather is good at fixing things. Anything from a broken toy to an old piece of furniture looks like new after it has visited his workshop. We have many things in our home proving his skill.

God is the most skilled craftsman of all. He changes the lives of men. Through Christ He reconciled us to Himself so that we can become new creatures. God is patient, working day after day to produce the best possible results in my life. Because I am the proof of His skill, I need to be sure I'm not misrepresenting Him to others.

Therefore, if anyone is in Christ, he is a new creation; the old has gone, the new has come! All this is from God, who reconciled us to himself through Christ and gave us the ministry of reconciliation (2 Cor. 5:17,18 NIV).

Thank You, Father, for making me into a new creature. I pray that others will know You by seeing the difference You've made in my life. Amen.

LOVE IS NOT BLIND

Of love, Rabbi Julius Gordon wrote these words:

Love is not blind — it sees more, not less.
But because it sees more, it is willing to see less.

This kind of love has its supreme example in God. He knows my faults better than anyone, yet He also loves me more than anyone else ever can. I too am called to this kind of love. If I find it hard to love someone, maybe I haven't seen enough of him or her to be willing to see less.

Bear with each other and forgive whatever grievances you may have against one another. Forgive as the Lord forgave you. And over all these virtues put on love, which binds them all together in perfect unity (Col. 3:13,14 NIV).

God, thank You for Your amazing love. Show me how to look at others through Your eyes, so I may grow in love and the ability to see fewer faults in them. Amen.

A TRAFFIC JAM

It was a hot day and our family was in the midst of a long line of cars that seemed to be standing still. The heat and slow pace of traffic made traveling miserable, but we knew it was useless to complain. Instead, we made up games to play. Progress was slow, but we kept going and were eventually on our way.

When we arrived at our destination that evening, the important thing wasn't the time it had taken, but how we had spent that time. Sometimes I want to go at a different pace than God has planned. I need to remember that how I live is more important than how fast I go.

But do not forget this one thing, dear friends: With the Lord a day is like a thousand years, and a thousand years are like a day (2 Peter 3:8 NIV).

Lord, too often I want to go at a different speed than the one that life demands. Thank You for being the traffic director for me to follow. Amen.

STRENGTH IN GENTLENESS

The harshest, cruelest street gangs make it to the "top." Leaders are considered greatest who act the toughest.

But actually these people are not truly strong individuals. It is the weak and insecure who feel a need to defend themselves. They try to prove to themselves and to others that they can handle anything. Only the strong can be gentle. They do not need to prove their strength or defend themselves. Christ is the best example of this. He's the greatest and He's also the most gentle. His Spirit provides the qualities of kindness, generosity, friendliness, and gentleness.

Your gentleness has made me great (2 Sam. 22:36 LB).

O Lord, grant that I will seek gentleness to prove my strength. Guide me in Your steps of greatness. Amen.

GROWING LOVE

A friend of mine often told me things about his father, whom he admired greatly. Even though I had never met the father personally, I began to think of him as a great person too.

Love for Jesus grows in the same way. Reading accounts in the Bible by those closest to Him, and hearing other Christians share His love, helps my love for Him to grow. This is how I can learn to know God best until that wonderful day when I will meet Him face to face.

I pray that out of his glorious riches he may strengthen you with power through his Spirit in your inner being, so that Christ may dwell in your hearts through faith (Eph. 3:16,17 NIV).

Heavenly Father, thank You for Your bountiful love shown to me through Your Word and Your servants. May I, too, show others Your love. Amen.

August 10

THE BOND IN JESUS

While on a vacation, a group of friends and I stopped at a little country church on Sunday morning. We felt at home immediately as the preacher introduced us to the rest of the congregation. After the service many came to talk to us individually, and we were invited several places for lunch.

Miles from home, we had found fellowship with others who were gathered for the same purpose — to worship God. They were our brothers and sisters even though we had never met before. It reminded me of the difference Jesus makes. Because of His love for each of His children, we can be united by that bond into fellowship with each other, no matter where or who we are.

And God placed all things under his feet and appointed him to be head over everything for the church, which is his body, the fullness of him who fills everything in every way (Eph. 1:22,23 NIV).

Thank You, Lord Jesus, for the bond that unifies all of Your children through Your love. Fellowship with You draws each into fellowship with one another. We are truly blessed. Amen.

DETOURS OF LIFE

Traveling down an interstate highway, we were suddenly forced to turn off the road by a detour sign. We didn't know the way on the new road, but we had to follow the signs anyway.

The back road was much more scenic than the highway. Even though we felt lost at first, we enjoyed the ride through the countryside. Eventually the signs led us back to the familiar road again.

Occasionally, God puts detour signs in my path to add extra spots of interest. I don't always appreciate being thrown off my course at first, and I feel lost; but when I follow the rest of His signs and come safely to the end, I can see the purpose of the detour.

God is my strong refuge, and has made my way safe (2 Sam. 22:33 RSV).

Thank You, Father, for the detours You place in my life that turn out so beautifully even when I'm skeptical at first. Teach me to follow Your signs. Amen.

THE PLANK IN MY EYE

It was a beautiful day. Many of our neighbors were taking advantage of the nice weather and had hung their wash outside to dry. Suddenly, with little warning, a cloudburst sent them all dashing out to rescue what was already wet. I chuckled to myself, glad that we had washed our clothes the day before.

When the rain was over, I remembered something that put an end to my smugness. I had slept outdoors the night before, and in the morning I'd hung my sleeping bag over the clothesline to air out. It was soaked. That taught me a good lesson to take a good look at myself before I laugh at others.

Why do you look at the speck of sawdust in your brother's eye and pay no attention to the plank in your own eye? (Matt. 7:3 NIV).

God, thank You for humorous ways of teaching me lessons. May I remember this lesson when I'm tempted to think others are worse off than I am. Amen.

August 13

GIVE

Robert J. McCracken, in one of his sermons, said:

> Love ever gives,
> Forgives, outlives,
> And ever stands
> With open hands.
> And while it lives,
> It gives.
> For this is love's prerogative —
> To give, and give, and give.

The giving spirit of love becomes evident as I look at those who love me. Those who truly love, don't think of what they will receive. They think only of how they can give more and more. This is the kind of love God commands me to have for each of His children.

But just as you excel in everything — in faith, in speech, in knowledge, in complete earnestness and in your love for us — see that you also excel in this grace of giving (2 Cor. 8:7 NIV).

Lord, be with me as I seek to love others. Teach me to give without expecting anything in return. Amen.

FRUIT-BEARING

A small cherry tree stands in the yard beside our house. When my brothers, sister, and I were younger we spent many hours in it, climbing its branches, swinging from the lowest boughs, and pretending to drive it as a car. Through all the abuse we gave the tree, it has continued to bear fruit each year.

The cherry tree has a powerful lesson to teach. The ungratefulness of others is not an adequate reason for me to stop bearing fruit. Jesus provides the necessary elements to continue growing in the fruit of His Spirit, even under abusive conditions.

This is to my Father's glory, that you bear much fruit, showing yourselves to be my disciples (John 15:8 NIV).

Thank You, Lord, for the strength to continue bearing fruit through the hardships others may give. Grant that I will be an encouragement to others to bear good fruit. Amen.

DON'T DESTROY — ENJOY!

Alongside nearly every road I travel, paper, tin cans, and other litter can be seen. Few rivers or streams are without debris humans have thrown away. The sky is filled with pollution.

Sometimes I wonder how God must feel about the way man is ruining His beautiful world. I do know one thing, however. Each person God sees who cares enough to do his part in cleaning up, or preventing further destruction, makes Him happy. I need to remember that the earth is God's gift to enjoy — not destroy.

The earth belongs to God! Everything in all the world is his! (Ps. 24:1 LB).

Father, thank You for this beautiful world to live in. Guide me in ways of conservation rather than destruction. Amen.

IN GOD'S LIGHT

Mornings are the most embarrassing times for someone who hasn't washed the windows recently. The bright sunlight shows clearly every dirty spot previously hidden by the darkness of the night.

That's how my life is. If I live in the darkness of sin, my ways don't appear to be bad. In fact, compared to others, they may seem good. But when I live in God's light, the flaws are easily seen. To perfect my life, I need to continue seeing it surrounded by God's righteousness.

I have come into the world as a light, so that no one who believes in me should stay in darkness (John 12:46 NIV).

Your light, my God, shines in the world to show up the evils of men. Thank You for shining in my life to show me what needs to be cleaned up. Amen.

PEARLS FROM SAND

The activities of an oyster beautifully illustrate the reactions Christians are to have to trouble. The oyster begins to work when a tiny piece of sand enters its shell. With great care, patience, and time, it builds layer after layer of a milky substance around the sand, covering each sharp corner. Eventually a pearl is formed around what was a problem to the oyster.

My natural instinct isn't to make each problem into something beautiful, but it's possible with God's grace.

And the Lord replied, "I myself will go with you and give you success" (Exod. 33:14 LB).

Be with me, Lord, as the sands of life come near me, that I may make them as beautiful as pearls. Amen.

THANK YOU

A few months ago I received a thank-you letter from the mother of one of my friends. It brightened my day, and even though I hadn't known her well before, I felt close to her because of her kind words. The time she took to write the letter meant a lot to me.

It made me think of how often I have many reasons to show my appreciation to friends and to God, but neglect doing anything. Appreciation, when given, strengthens the relationship. If I feel far away from God, I should think of things I'm thankful for and tell Him about them.

It is good to say, "Thank you" to the Lord, to sing praises to the God who is above all gods (Ps. 92:1 LB).

Gracious Father, teach me the full meaning of thanksgiving. May I learn to show my praise and gratitude more often. Thank You for giving me so much to be thankful for. Amen.

August 19

WORKING TOGETHER FOR GOOD

Some time ago, I decided to spend a short vacation with one of my friends. I considered various ways to get there, but nothing was working out. I felt God was shutting the doors to me, so I decided not to go.

Then I was given a rare opportunity to go somewhere else during that time, where I was greatly enriched. A couple months later, God provided me with another chance to visit my friend. Both experiences, as well as seeing God work in a beautiful way, added so much to my life.

Paul knew what he was talking about when he said that "all things work together for good to them that love God."

Yet not as I will, but as you will (Matt. 26:39 NIV).

Thank You, God, for directing me in the ways You know to be best. Why would I ever want to neglect finding Your will? Amen.

August 20

NO INSTANT REPLAY

One of the miracles of the modern camera is instant replay. Only minutes after an exciting play has taken place in a game or event, it can be seen again.

Life cannot be replayed like that. A bad day can never be taken back and a good day can never be done over. I cannot live on yesterdays. Each day must be new with fresh vitality. I can only retain the beauty by seeing each day as a new gift from God and thanking Him for it.

I will praise you, my God and King, and bless your name each day and forever (Ps. 145:1 LB).

Thank You, my God and King, for this beautiful day to praise You anew. May I see each day as a new gift from You to use for Your glory. Amen.

August 21

BE READY

I once read of a man who said that he was waiting till his last moment to give his life to Christ. He wanted to live his own life on earth, but he wanted to spend eternity with Jesus in heaven.

His way of thinking seems foolish. Besides missing the blessings and joy of living with Christ now, he may never know that joy. Jesus doesn't always let us recognize our last moments. He says that we are to be ready at all times.

So you also must be ready, because the Son of Man will come at an hour when you do not expect him (Matt. 24:44 NIV).

Dear Lord, I thank You that it's not important for me to know when my last moments will be. I need to be ready all the time. Amen.

August 22

A PROMISE KEEPER

Early in childhood, I realized that whatever my parents told me was the truth. They never lied to me, and they kept their promises.

This helped me to trust in God as I grew older. God has made many promises in the Bible. By seeing humans keep their promises, I can have faith that God, through Christ, will keep His promises.

For no matter how many promises God has made, they are "Yes" in Christ (2 Cor. 1:20 NIV).

Father, teach me to know Your ways and rely on Your promises. Thank You for human examples of Your trust. Amen.

August 23

ON THE ROCK

A friend and I sat on a large rock, watching the river swirl swiftly past. We felt secure in the fact that as long as we stayed on that firm rock, we were safe. Many other rocks were nearby, but they seemed more unstable, slippery, and dangerous, so we stayed where we were.

Watching the water flow past gave me a sense of peace, as if nothing else mattered. Staying on the rock kept me from being pulled downstream with the current.

In life, with Christ as the Rock, the same thing is true. I can be at peace, knowing that even though everything around me is unsteady, when I depend on Jesus to hold me up, I don't have to be afraid of being swept along by other forces.

Yes, he alone is my Rock, my rescuer, defense and fortress. Why then should I be tense with fear when troubles come? (Ps. 62:2 LB).

You are my Rock, Lord, on whom I can depend when life seems to swirl too fast around me. Thank You. Amen.

JESUS WEPT

In our culture crying is considered a sign of weakness. No one, particularly males, should ever be caught crying.

Jesus, the strongest and most gentle person who ever lived, wasn't afraid to cry. His tears showed the love He had for Lazarus, His friend who had died. I need to form a new attitude toward crying. Tears can be a sign of great love instead of weakness. I should thank God for providing a release for my hurts or compassion for others, rather than trying to hold them in.

Jesus wept. Then the Jews said, "See how he loved him!" (John 11:35,36 NIV).

Thank You, Jesus, for Your example and for my freedom to shed tears of love and compassion without shame. Amen.

REACHING THE GOAL

I like the story of a girl who had three suitors. She suggested they run a race, and the one who caught her would be her husband.

She filled her pockets with money, and they all began to run. As the first suitor came close to her, she dropped some money in his path. As he stopped to pick it up, she escaped. The same thing happened to her second pursuer.

The money did not dissuade the third young man, however. He continued running and caught the girl for his wife. He treasured her above the money.

Like the last suitor, I must not be sidetracked by anything that may be put in my path which keeps me from reaching my goal. Only by continuing the race will I win the prize.

I press on toward the goal to win the prize for which God has called me heavenward in Christ Jesus (Phil. 3:14 NIV).

Guide me in the race to You, Father, that I may always keep my goal in You. Amen.

THANK YOU, GOD

My sister has a devotional book that has space after each day's meditation to write a prayer. In reading several of the prayers she has written, I noticed that most of her sentences began with, "Thank you. . . ." Knowing of some rough times she had had, I turned to those days. To my surprise, I found only praise in the midst of those troubles. I have remembered those prayers since the day I read them, and they have been a continual inspiration to me. I, too, can find something to praise God for in every situation, if I'm willing to try.

I will praise you, my God and King, and bless your name each day and forever (Ps. 145:1 LB).

Thank You, my God, for my sister and the influence her attitude has had on me. Thank You for giving me something to praise You for every day of my life. Amen.

HIS HANDS

It was a great day when I was first asked to baby-sit for several children. I felt honored that the parents trusted me enough to go away, having confidence that I would take good care of their children.

It was a much greater day when Jesus returned to heaven. Before He left, He put His work on earth into the hands of His followers. They were to continue it for Him, to function as His hands, feet, ears, and heart on earth.

He still calls me, as one of His disciples, to do His work. I should consider it a great privilege to be trusted to care for the unsaved of the world.

> **Therefore go and make disciples of all nations, baptizing them in the name of the Father and of the Son and of the Holy Spirit, and teaching them to obey everything I have commanded you (Matt. 28:19,20 NIV).**

Lord, let me be a tool for Your ministry. Thank You for giving me the great responsibility of being a worker for You. Amen.

August 28

ENCOURAGEMENT ON THE HILLS

Climbing a steep hill, I was relieved to meet a friend who stopped for awhile to talk. Not only was the conversation refreshing, but it also gave me a chance to rest before continuing the hard climb.

The road of life is sometimes steep too. It is a beautiful thing to have friends who encourage me by stopping to talk. It is also beautiful when I can provide a rest spot and brighten someone else's climb.

> **Two can accomplish more than twice as much as one, for the results can be much better. If one falls, the other pulls him up (Eccl. 4:9,10 LB).**

Direct me, Master, in paths that cross with others', so I may refresh them on their way. Thank You for the daily opportunities to shine for You. Amen.

JESUS IS THE WAY

Bees are interesting creatures. When one bee finds a field of flowers, it returns to the hive and flies in a certain pattern. From this, the other bees know which direction the field is in and exactly how far away it is.

God sent Jesus into the world to tell us where the greatest gift on earth is and how to receive it. The only way to know God is through His Son. When I look to Jesus, He leads me to the treasure of life, both now and hereafter.

Jesus answered, "I am the way — and the truth and the life. No one comes to the Father except through me" (John 14:6 NIV).

Thank You, Father, for sending Your Son to show me the way to You. Be with me as I follow His leading. Amen.

FRUITFUL IN CHRIST

When we returned from our vacation, I ran to check my row of cantaloupe. I had spent many hours watering and weeding the plants, and now the fruit should be almost ripe. When I got to them, however, I was disappointed to find that in my absence, our duck had waddled straight down the middle of the row, breaking and killing many vines.

Christ must suffer many times when He nurtures a person's growth, and then something destroys the vines of communication and fellowship. Without being connected to Christ I can't bear the fruit of His Spirit.

Remain in me, and I will remain in you. No branch can bear fruit by itself; it must remain in the vine. Neither can you bear fruit unless you remain in me (John 15:4 NIV).

Grant, O Lord, that nothing will sever the vines of communication connecting us, so that I will bear much fruit. Thank You for being the Vine. Amen.

August 31

GIFTS

The following words by Francis Maitland Balfour have a lot of meaning in them. If I practice what they say, my life will be joyful.

The best thing to give to your enemy is forgiveness; to an opponent, tolerance; to a friend, your heart; to your child, a good example; to your father, deference; to your mother, conduct that will make her proud of you; to yourself, respect; to all men, charity.

And now these three remain: faith, hope and love. But the greatest of these is love (1 Cor. 13:13 NIV).

Dear God, help me to know what it is to love all men, forgive my enemy, and to be a good example to others, as You have done. Amen.

CHRIST, MY PILOT

I remember seeing a reproduction of Warner Sallman's painting "Christ, Our Pilot." In the painting, a young man is steering his boat through stormy waters. The sky is dark with clouds, pierced by streaks of lightning. Jesus' presence is portrayed standing behind the youth, with one hand on his shoulder and the other pointing forward. Jesus is not taking over the helm, but simply shows the way and remains by his side to give him comfort.

At my invitation, Christ becomes the Pilot of my life. He doesn't force me to go a certain way, but He patiently shows me the best route. I must follow Him in faith.

The apostle said to the Lord, "Increase our faith!" (Luke 17:5 NIV).

Thank You, God, for being my Guide and Protector in the course of life. I pray that I will never be satisfied as my own pilot. Amen.

PULLING WEEDS OF SIN

From experience with pulling weeds in our garden, I know that the older and bigger a weed is, the harder it is to pull out. Sometimes one is rooted so deep that pulling it out almost knocks me over.

Weeds of sin are also easier to pull out before they have a chance to dig their roots deep into my life. I must keep after them constantly. Even though I may not enjoy dealing with my sins, it's necessary in keeping my life clean. Sin becomes harder to uproot the longer I wait.

So let us put aside the deeds of darkness and put on the armor of light (Rom. 13:12 NIV).

You are the perfect Gardener, O Lord. Help me to keep the weeds of sin out of my life. Amen.

September 3

GOD'S EVERLASTING LOVE

Each of my trials has an end, even though some of them seem to last a long time. God's love continues, however, and helps me through everything. I like the poem by P. Gerhardt that says:

> All my life I still have found,
>   And I will forget it never,
> Every sorrow hath its bound,
>   And no cross endures forever.
> All things else have but their day,
> God's love only lasts for aye.

He will not break the bruised reed, nor quench the dimly burning flame. He will encourage the faint-hearted, those tempted to despair (Isa. 42:3 LB).

Thank You, God, for Your love that covers every trial and sorrow I have. Amen.

September 4

AGLOW WITH GOD'S PRESENCE

As I watched and listened to the preacher before me, I suddenly realized why he had become a favorite of mine. Not only did he speak of joy in Christ, but the radiance on his face also spoke of that joy. I knew by looking at him that Christ's Spirit filled his heart.

After the service, I shared with him my appreciation for his happy face. To my surprise, he admitted that he didn't realize he was smiling during the sermon. It was another example to me of what Christ can do if I give Him total control.

> **Moses didn't realize as he came back down the mountain with the tablets that his face glowed from being in the presence of God (Exod. 34:29 LB).**

Father, I pray that I too will glow with the Spirit of Your presence. Thank You for being so real. Amen.

September 5

FREEDOM OF CHOICE

How well I remember the free feeling of being away from home for the first time. I was enjoying a week of summer camp, free to do anything without worrying about what my parents would say.

I soon made a discovery. When exercising my new freedom, I found that I could only be happy by thinking of my parents' wishes. Jesus also gives me freedom to choose what I will do. I've found, however, that I can be truly happy only when I'm in His will.

> **Live as free men, but do not use your freedom as a cover-up for evil; live as servants of God (1 Peter 2:16 NIV).**

Thank You, Jesus, for the freedom of choice You have given me. Guide me in using the freedom for Your glory. Amen.

IT TAKES TIME

Not much of Jesus' life between the ages of twelve and thirty is revealed. He probably spent a lot of time with His heavenly Father, learning the many things necessary for His three years of ministry.

The disciples also spent time in training. They followed, observed, and questioned Jesus for three years before they were sent out on their own to minister. I'm sometimes too anxious to know everything right away. I must remember that it takes time to learn the ways of Jesus.

"Come, follow me," Jesus said, "and I will make you fishers of men" (Matt. 4:19 NIV).

Give me patience, Jesus, to follow You, learning things as You teach me. Thank You for Your example. Amen.

TUNE UP

I watched as a man tuned our piano. Notes that sounded all right to me didn't satisfy him, so he worked until every note was perfectly in tune. Since he was a better musician than I, he was better able to tell that the piano was out of tune.

When I'm tempted to think my life is sinless and good, maybe I'm not sensitive enough to what is good and bad. As the musician must have a good ear to tune instruments, I must develop a good conscience to tune my life to Christ.

Do not be overcome by evil, but overcome evil with good (Rom. 12:21 NIV).

Teach me, Lord, to know when my life is out of tune with Your will. Help me to develop a good conscience to guide me. Amen.

GOD WORKS THROUGH THE ORDINARY

Sometimes when I'm working at home I wish I could be doing more than the regular chores of a household. Then I'm reminded of the story of Rebekah, found in Genesis, which helps me to be satisfied with whatever I'm doing.

As she was performing her usual chore of drawing water from the well, she was asked for a drink. Her willingness and kindness changed the rest of her life. What I'm doing isn't always as important as what kind of an attitude I have. God works through ordinary things too.

Then she said, "I'll draw water for your camels, too, until they have enough!" (Gen. 24:19 LB).

Thank You, God, that I can be assured of Your guidance in all the activities of my life. Amen.

CONTROL OF NEW EXPERIENCES

I watched as my brother trained his horse for riding. To get the horse accustomed to weight, my brother put bags of sand on her back. Many days later he saddled her. After more waiting and training, my brother was finally able to mount.

When Jesus rode into Jerusalem, he sat on an unbroken colt. That in itself was a miracle. He had complete control of the colt when the crowd was yelling, throwing clothes down for it to walk on, and waving palm branches. If Jesus was able to keep that colt calm, I can trust Him to keep me calm and guide me in new experiences.

Go to the village ahead of you, and just as you enter it, you will find a colt tied there, which no one has ever ridden (Mark 11:2 NIV).

Lord, I want the same strong hands that calmed the colt on the way to Jerusalem to be my guide on the way to my heavenly home. Amen.

September 10

LEARNING TO LOVE

As the teacher read the new seating chart, I found myself sitting beside a girl I hardly knew. I had never talked to her, and from the start I knew she wouldn't be easy to love. Her impatience caused her to have few friends.

As I learned more about her throughout the year and became her friend, I saw reasons why patience was especially hard for her. I wondered if I could have been even as patient as she was, considering the circumstances she lived with.

Christ didn't tell me to love only those whom I understand. Sometimes I must first show kindness; and then He will show me why they were hard to love.

Follow God's example in everything you do just as a much loved child imitates his father. Be full of love for others (Eph. 5:1,2 LB).

When I don't understand someone, Father, give me patience to love that person anyway. Maybe a friend is just what he or she needs. Thank You for Your example. Amen.

ICEBERGS AND PEOPLE

Like the person I mentioned yesterday, I have become friends with some people I didn't appreciate much at first. I have learned that people are like icebergs. The little bit that is seen doesn't nearly begin to portray all that lies beneath the surface.

Shy people are like that. At first there doesn't seem to be much to them because they aren't easy to get to know. But when I'm willing to spend time with them and dig deeper for meaning, each person becomes unique and beautiful in his own way. If a person seems uninteresting, it's probably because I don't know him or her well enough yet.

Accept one another, then, just as Christ accepted you, in order to bring praise to God (Rom. 15:7 NIV).

Give me the patience, Lord, to learn to know people before I judge their worth. Teach me to look deep enough to see their beauty. Amen.

STRONG BUILDERS FOR CHRIST

Two of my uncles are housing contractors, and they know the importance of precise work. If they would build carelessly, even though others may not notice at first, after several years things would start falling apart. Their good reputations and jobs would be lost.

All of life can be compared to building a house. Every thought, act, and decision I make is being added to the construction of my life and determines what kind of a building I construct. Even if I try to hide the bad parts, God knows the difference and will not allow them to stand. I need to keep in mind that each choice I make helps to decide how strong my house is becoming.

For God will judge us for everything we do, including every hidden thing, good or bad (Eccl. 12:14 LB).

Thank You, God, for the reminder that each step I take in building my life must be precise. Guide me in each decision. Amen.

September 13

BEFORE I ASK

When I meet new friends who become especially close to me, I sometimes think about the fact that God gave them to me before I asked Him for anyone. He knows my need and provides for it before I realize the need myself. It's a good feeling to know that in a world where each person is expected to take care of himself, I have a Protector who takes care of me better than I ever could myself.

And I will also give you what you didn't ask for — riches and honor! (1 Kings 3:13 LB).

Thank You, Lord, for supplying needs in my life that I may not even be aware of. You are truly a great and wonderful God. Amen.

September 14

LOVE NOTES

The first months in a new school, with new classmates and teachers, can be lonely at times. That was my experience when I transferred to a different high school. An event that has stayed in my memory is the note that a classmate gave me one day. What she said wasn't especially important, but just knowing that she cared enough to spend time to let me know it was a tremendous lift!

She and other friends have continued writing these short "love notes," and each time it makes my whole day better! I've found that an even greater blessing is to give to others. A note of sincere appreciation is well worth the little bit of time it takes to write it.

Therefore, encourage one another and build each other up (1 Thess. 5:11 NIV).

Lord, thank You for friends. Show me someone today whose life I could brighten by a love note of encouragement and appreciation. Amen.

September 15

BUILDING CHARACTER

When pure gold and pure silver are pressed together, even for a short time, part of each is buried in the other. Unless they're put under a microscope, that fact is often unnoticeable.

People are like that too. I receive bits from each person I touch with my presence, and part of me is imbedded in them. It may not be immediately evident, but it's still there.

I can choose what kind of bits I want to plant in others, by guarding my thoughts and actions to what will help to strengthen others. I'm responsible for the part of me in other people, as well as what I allow to be rubbed off from them to me.

Let us therefore make every effort to do what leads to peace and to mutual edification (Rom. 14:19 NIV).

Lord, guide my ways that I will always seek to edify those I come in contact with. Amen.

REST

Rest is not quitting
  The busy career;
Rest is the fitting
  Of self to its sphere.
'Tis loving and serving
  The highest and best!
'Tis onwards, unswerving —
  And that is true rest.

— J. S. Dwight

I used to think of rest as laziness or inaction; but as Dwight has helped me to understand, rest is inner peace and quiet. It feels and acts in God's will. Rest is more than a break from work. It is a whole dimension of life.

Now we who have believed enter that rest (Heb. 4:3 NIV).

I give myself to You, God, to do Your will. Then I may also rest in Your peace. Amen.

September 17

KEEP EXERCISING

I once heard of an elderly man who jogged a mile every morning to maintain his good health. He had exercised in this way every day for years, and he knew that if he wanted to stay in shape, he couldn't stop.

I need to exercise the fruit of the Holy Spirit in my life each day to stay in shape. I can never be content to have reached a certain maturity in my Christian life and then stop exercising. I can stay healthy in Christ only by exercising His Word in my life each day.

> **Therefore, since we are surrounded by such a great cloud of witnesses, let us throw off everything that hinders and the sin that so easily entangles, and let us run with perseverance the race marked out for us (Heb. 12:1 NIV).**

Keep me mindful, Lord, of the daily exercise I need to stay in shape with You. Thank You for giving me strength to stay healthy in You. Amen.

September 18

MAKING FRIENDS CAN BE HARD

When I was younger, dad had a job in which he traveled a lot. On some of his shorter trips, our family accompanied him. This meant meeting many new people. Until I learned to know someone in the new surroundings, it was awkward. But the rewarding times came too. It often became difficult to part with a new friend. Meeting people can be frightening, but by keeping a few things in mind, it can be fun:

1) The other person is probably just as shy as I am, so someone might as well make the first move — why not me?
2) We probably have at least one thing in common — I should take time to find out what it is.
3) The sooner I get to know that person, the longer I'll have to be with him or her and enjoy the new-found friendship.

I don't want to miss out on an exciting relationship just because I'm too shy to say "hi."

Love your neighbor as yourself (Rom. 13:9 NIV).

Thank You, Lord, for so many beautiful people. Thank You, too, for opportunities to learn to know more of Your sons and daughters who help me feel closer to You. Amen.

TO FIND THE LOST

I remember well the day we lost our new dog. The whole family and many neighbors became concerned. We spent hours searching the woods and driving around looking for him. Many phone calls were made to alert people to be on the lookout for him. Finally, in the evening, he was found. Our friends and neighbors rejoiced with us over his appearance.

How much greater is the rejoicing over one sinner who leaves his sinful life behind and makes his appearance in God's kingdom!

Then he calls his friends and neighbors together and says, "Rejoice with me; I have found my lost sheep" (Luke 15:6 NIV).

O Lord, give me concern for those who haven't found their home in You. Show me ways I can help them find You. Amen.

THE GREATEST INHERITANCE

When my grandparents moved to a smaller house, they gathered their children together to give them many of their possessions. They gave away dishes, furniture, and books they had collected over the years that would now find use in their children's families.

God has been preparing a kingdom for His children ever

since He created the earth. He looks forward to the day when He will call them all together to present them with His gift of eternal life. My hope is in the day I will be able to claim my share in this tremendous inheritance.

Come, you who are blessed by my Father: take your inheritance, the kingdom prepared for you since the creation of the world (Matt. 25:34 NIV).

Thank You, Father, for the inheritance of Your kingdom which I have the privilege of sharing in. Amen.

September 21

GOD KNOWS ALL

At a party I was taken out of the room where my friends were and was told that we were playing a game. When I went back, I was led to the center of the circle. Not a word was said, but everyone stared at me. They seemed to look right through me, and I soon became so uncomfortable that I left the room again. Then they explained that they merely wanted to see my reactions to the staring and silence.

God is always watching me, and He knows everything I do, say, or think. I must be careful to do only what I won't feel guilty for on that final day when God looks straight at me, knowing everything.

There is nothing concealed that will not be disclosed, or hidden that will not be made known. What you have said in the dark will be heard in the daylight, and what you have whispered in the ear behind closed doors will be proclaimed from the housetops (Luke 12:2,3 NIV).

O God, guide me in the ways You want me to go, so I don't need to be afraid to let my words or actions be heard or seen. Thank You for the strength I know You can give. Amen.

RESPONSIBILITY IN LOVE

The trailer my cousin was sleeping in caught on fire one night. Being a heavy sleeper, she didn't wake up at first, but her dog jumped on her again and again until she realized what was happening. He may have saved her life.

Many people are sleeping today, unaware of how little time they have to wake up and leave their life of wrong-doing. They may resent being bothered at first, but if I have enough love, I will keep trying to awaken them. When I see the best way and my neighbors haven't seen it yet, it's my responsibility to show it to them.

Love your neighbor as yourself (Luke 10:27 NIV).

Give me enough love, Father, to want to share what I have experienced with my neighbor. Thank You for Your sustaining love. Amen.

FALSE PROPHETS

While visiting a wax museum, I was never sure if a person was real or just made of wax. The artists of the wax figures made them look so lifelike that I smiled at the guard, only to realize when he didn't smile back that he was wax.

Jesus said that's how false prophets are. They look like something they're not. I must remember that everyone who speaks of God hasn't necessarily been sent by Him.

Watch our for false prophets. They come to you in sheep's clothing, but inwardly they are ferocious wolves (Matt. 7:15 NIV).

Thank You, Jesus, for Your words of warning. Give me direction in discerning words of truth. Amen.

BY THEIR FRUITS

I watched many figures in the wax museum. I had learned that I couldn't be sure they were real until I saw them move or speak.

So it is with false prophets. I can't be sure people are prophets of God until I observe Christlike qualities in them. Blindly following anyone who claims to be from God is unwise. I must learn to test what I hear with what I know from the Scriptures. The responsibility is mine to question whether or not a prophet has the fruit of living under the lordship of Christ.

> **By their fruit you will recognize them. . . . A good tree cannot bear bad fruit, and a bad tree cannot bear good fruit (Matt. 7:16,18 NIV).**

Remind me, Father, to always question what kind of fruit a prophet has before blindly following. Thank You for Your guidance. Amen.

SUNSHINE MAKES SHADOWS

A friend shared an experience she had while flying above the clouds in an airplane. The sun was shining brightly around her, but when she looked down between the clouds, she noticed that the clouds were blocking the sun. Even though the sun was shining above, the people below couldn't see it. The clouds under the sun produced dark shadows on the ground.

When dark times come, instead of complaining about the clouds that cause the shadows, I need to realize that the sun is still shining beyond the clouds. Shadows can't exist without the light, and sunshine sometimes produces shadows to bring awareness of its light.

I have learned the secret of being content in any and every situation, whether well-fed or hungry, whether living in plenty or in want (Phil. 4:12 NIV).

Thank You, Lord, for Your light. When it produces shadows in my life, teach me to realize that sunshine is near — just beyond the clouds. Amen.

GOD IS DEPENDABLE

Wondering how many times a day parents are called on by their children, I listened closely to the activities of our home for one day. I heard everything from "Mom, where's my shirt?" to "Dad, will you take me shopping?" with countless other emergencies in between. We knew without thinking about it that our parents would listen and help in the best way they knew how.

God is even more dependable than my earthly parents. He is always ready to listen and will answer my prayers. All I need to do is ask. I should learn to talk to God as naturally as I talk to the people I live with.

If you, then, though you are evil, know how to give good gifts to your children, how much more will your Father in heaven give good gifts to those who ask him! (Matt. 7:11 NIV).

God, thank You for always being near and hearing my prayers. May I learn to talk to You more naturally throughout my daily tasks. Amen.

HIS LOVE CONTINUES

Another thing I have discovered about the parent-child relationship is that most of the time it's the child who is asking for something. If the parents do something right, they are usually left without a word of praise. But if they do something wrong, they are sure to be reminded of it. Amazingly, their love continues.

Too often I only communicate with my heavenly Father when something goes wrong. I forget to praise Him for a job well done. It's amazing how His love for me continues when I keep asking for more and forget to say, "I love You, Father."

I love the Lord because he hears my prayers and answers them (Ps. 116:1 LB).

Forgive me, heavenly Father, when I continually ask for things and forget to praise You for them. I love You. Amen.

CHOOSING FRIENDS

High school was a time when I made social breaks from my family and began to spend more time with other people. Some people seem easier to get to know than others, but to really know anyone takes time.

One particular friend and I knew each other a year before we could share our real feelings. She had always reminded me of the typical all-American teen-ager — happy, efficient, always ready to help, good looking, with just about everything going for her. As we grew closer, I realized that she was the same as everyone else. She had her share of rough times, too.

Other relationships are similar. Learning to really know people and being able to share with them of my deepest convictions are where the true riches in life are found. My choice of friends will determine the kind of life I live.

A mirror reflects a man's face, but what he is really like is shown by the kind of friends he chooses (Prov. 27:19 LB).

Father, guide me in choosing my friends – ones who bring me closer to You. May I be the kind of friend to others that You want me to be. Amen.

LONELY PEOPLE

There was a nursing home just down the road from where I lived, so some friends and I took the opportunity to visit some of its lonely residents. Glenn, the man I chose to visit, was ninety-four years old and spent most of his time in bed.

Some weeks when I went to his room, he told me stories of his past. Sometimes he complained about his failing health. At other times we shared silences. Each time, when I stood to leave, he told me how much my visits meant to him.

What we talked about wasn't as important to him as knowing someone cared about him. I'll never be sorry for the time I've spent with a lonely person. I may be sorry, however, that I haven't done it more.

The King will reply, "I tell you the truth, whatever you did for one of the least of these brothers of mine, you did for me" (Matt. 25:40 NIV).

Thank You, Lord, for the opportunities I have to be a friend to lonely people. I pray that I will make use of these times to spread Your love and care. Amen.

SAD IN LOVE

My newest griefs to Thee are old;
   My last transgression of Thy law,
Though wrapped in thoughts most
     secret fold,
   Thine eyes with pitying sadness saw.

These words of H. M. Kimball portray a God of compassion. When I sin against His laws, God isn't angry, thinking of revenge. He is sad, thinking only of love.

When I sin, I almost wish God would be harsh. Then I'd feel I got what I deserved. But God is love. In love I want to do only that which makes Him happy, not sad.

May my spoken words and unspoken thoughts be pleasing even to You, O Lord, my Rock and my Redeemer (Ps. 19:14 LB).

Forgive me, Father, for the times I've made You sad. I want to do only what makes You happy. Amen.

FLEXIBILITY NEEDED

I once heard someone say that the reason the Constitution of the United States has been useful for so long is because of its tremendous flexibility. It reminded me that in our changing world, my mind needs to be flexible also to be useful.

The Bible never changes, but I must always read it with a mind open to change. God will reveal new truths to me if my mind is flexible enough to hear His voice over stubborn beliefs and wrongdoings.

I am listening carefully to all the Lord is saying — for he speaks peace to his people, his saints, if they will only stop their sinning (Ps. 85:8 LB).

Thank You, God, for Your stable Word. Give me an attitude of flexibility that is willing to change when You show me a new truth. Amen.

ALWAYS MORE

I like the story in 1 Kings of the woman who had enough faith to feed Elijah her last handful of flour and last drops of oil, even though she and her son faced starvation. Because she obeyed God, she had as much as she needed. Her flour and oil never ran out.

I have never known what it is to have as little as this woman, but I wonder if I'd be as willing to give as she was. It's sometimes hard to give, even out of my plenty. This story teaches a powerful lesson. God rewards those who listen to Him, even if His commands don't always seem sensible.

For no matter how much they used, there was always plenty left in the containers, just as the Lord had promised through Elijah! (1 Kings 17:16 LB).

Lord, thank You for all that You've given to me. Grant that I will always be willing to give even if it means less for me. Amen.

October 3

LEAVES AND OTHER BLESSINGS

Last fall I received a letter from a friend who lived in the deserts of Arizona. He told me of a weekend retreat he had attended that was held in the distant Rocky Mountains. The highlight of the weekend for him seemed to be seeing the beauty of the red, orange, and yellow autumn leaves, and hearing them crunch underfoot.

Having lived in the mountains of Virginia, the fall leaves were commonplace for me, and many times as I shuffled through them, I hardly noticed their beauty. My friend's letter reminded me of the many gifts God has provided for my enjoyment.

I want to express publicly before his people my heartfelt thanks to God for his mighty miracles. All who are thankful should ponder them with me (Ps. 111:1,2 LB).

Thank You, Father, for beautiful autumn leaves and the many other blessings You have given me, waiting only for my appreciation. Amen.

October 4

GOD WAITS

Hearing the crunch of dried leaves under my feet, feeling the crisp wind nip my nose as it rushes by, and watching the squirrels gather acorns for the winter are only a few signs of autumn that put excitement in the air. It's as if nature has a secret that she whispers to anyone who is willing to stop and listen.

It reminds me of the way God speaks. He lets me know of His presence in the things and people around me, then He waits for me to stop and listen to the secrets of His heart. Not only in autumn, but every day of the year, I need to listen for His voice.

Come near to God and he will come near to you (James 4:8 NIV).

Thank You, God, for Your patience. Grant me awareness of Your waiting voice when I forget to stop and listen. Amen.

October 5

LOOK STRAIGHT AHEAD

Watching a horse pull a cart along the road, I noticed that blinders had been fastened on its head so it could only see straight ahead. They prevented the horse from being distracted by activities at the sides.

Sometimes I think it might be good if I could attach something to myself to prevent me from being distracted along the road to eternal life. It's often tempting to look behind or beside me instead of keeping my eyes on God. To reach my goal, I must only look forward and keep moving in that direction.

Submit yourselves, then, to God. Resist the devil, and he will flee from you (James 4:7 NIV).

Lord, help me to continue to look to You, even when distractions are tempting me to go in another direction. Thank You for leading me. Amen.

TURNING THE OTHER CHEEK

As a child, I remember times when one of us children would put on the "holier than thou" attitude for awhile, and turn the other cheek instead of hitting back. The rest would take advantage of the situation and hit the other cheek too. We were taking Matthew 5:39 literally. I believe Jesus had more meaning in those words than I understood then. Now I see it as an illustration used to teach the proper attitude I should have toward those who hurt me. I must be willing to take hurt without wishing anything bad for the one who hurt me. With Jesus' help, I can forgive and forget without thought of retaliation.

But I tell you, Do not resist an evil person. If someone strikes you on the right cheek, turn to him the other also (Matt. 5:39 NIV).

Forgive me, Jesus, for the times when I haven't taken hurt without retaliation like You told me to. Help me to be more sensitive to Your Spirit. Thank You. Amen.

SOAR HIGH

A rare species of cormorants live on the Galapagos Islands. They have wings but they can't fly. They have no enemies to fly from and they can obtain their food on foot, so they have no need to fly.

This creature is typical of some people. By failure to use their God-given abilities, they soar no higher in the spiritual realm. By remaining in secular society, they forget the beauty and excitement of lifting their lives to higher and better experiences.

Do not neglect your gift (1 Tim. 4:14 NIV).

Thank You, dear God, for abilities You have given to me. Teach me to use them so I don't lose them. Amen.

USING AVAILABLE TOOLS

Another animal on the Galapagos Islands is a small bird called the woodpecker finch. Its distinguishing feature is that it is the only living creature, besides man, that uses a tool. It digs insects out of holes with twigs that it breaks off trees.

The woodpecker finch is typical of some people. It has learned to use tools that are available for survival. Similarly, many people use the tools of learning for personal growth. God helps me grow when I make use of what I already have.

Be diligent in these matters; give yourself wholly to them, so that everyone may see your progress (1 Tim. 4:15 NIV).

Teach me, Lord, to recognize the tools available to me to use in my personal growth. Amen.

BEING LESS CRITICAL

An Indian prayer that I've seen on the shelf in dad's study says, "Grant that I may not criticize my neighbor until I have walked a mile in his moccasins." It is a good reminder to me. Too often I'm tempted to criticize people before I know everything they are going through. Instead of thinking negatively of others, I should thank God that I haven't had to experience the same things they are experiencing.

You, then, why do you judge your brother? Or why do you look down on your brother? (Rom. 14:10 NIV).

Forgive me, Father, for times I have criticized others. Help me to be more sensitive to their needs instead of to their faults. Amen.

A NEW HOUSE

A house in our neighborhood was so run-down and dilapidated that no one wanted to live in it. Then a couple decided to buy it and fix it up. They saw hope in what others saw only as ruin. When they finished remodeling, the house looked like new.

My life is like that house. Before I gave it to Jesus, it was torn up and on its way to being ruined in sin. But when I gave Christ the ownership, I was transformed into a new person. I pray He will never stop making repairs, adding new rooms, and making any other necessary improvements on my "house."

I stand at the door and knock. If anyone hears my voice and opens the door, I will go in and eat with him, and he with me (Rev. 3:20 NIV).

I'm so happy You saw something worth fixing in my life, Jesus, instead of giving me up as hopeless. Thank You for all the work You're doing in me. Amen.

FREEDOM TO CHOOSE

Sometimes when I pray for the salvation of one of my friends, God doesn't seem to be answering. I want Him to perform some miracle so my friend will immediately want to serve Him.

God, however, doesn't manipulate anyone's life. Instead of controlling me like a puppet, He has given me and everyone else a freedom to choose. God will help me to influence others with my life, but I can only make decisions for myself. I must, therefore, ask God to guide me in ways of showing His love to those around me.

This is good, and pleases God our Savior, who wants all men to be saved and to come to a knowledge of the truth (1 Tim. 2:3,4 NIV).

O mighty God, I realize that even though You want all men to be saved, You don't manipulate them. Show me ways I can be an effective influence for You. Amen.

October 12

BLOOM WHERE YOU ARE PLANTED

"Bloom where you are planted." Those words were proclaimed from the showcase at school in big, colorful letters. I thought it was a beautiful reminder of my responsibility to be happy in whatever situation I am placed.

When I'm planted in happy surroundings, it's easy to bloom; but tense and tough situations make it difficult. Nevertheless, the words remain: "Bloom where you are planted." I learned that the challenge isn't to bloom only when I'm planted in good surroundings, but to continue blooming in bad situations as well.

In every way we show ourselves to be servants of God: in great endurance; in troubles, hardships and distresses (2 Cor. 6:4 NIV).

Thank You, Father, for giving me strength to bloom wherever I'm planted. May I continue to draw nourishment from You. Amen.

SHARING TROUBLES

When my younger brother was taken to the hospital for several days, God's love shone through to our family in many ways. Friends and neighbors brought meals to us, took some of my parents' responsibilities, and assured us of their prayers. They truly shared our troubles as Paul commended the Philippians for sharing his. Knowing how much this was appreciated, it became an incentive to me to share the troubles of others in material ways or in prayer.

Yet it was good of you to share in my troubles (Phil. 4:14 NIV).

Thank You, Lord, for brothers and sisters who follow Your way of sharing my troubles. They make You more real. Amen.

THE INTERCESSOR

Sometimes people get facts mixed up when they're praying, and I find myself correcting them in my mind. Usually I know what they mean, but they probably don't realize what they have said. It makes me wonder how often I don't realize how I'm praying and thus ask for the wrong things.

It's a blessing to know that when I want to follow God's will, the Holy Spirit intercedes for me and straightens out my prayers. He understands thoughts I can't express in words and tells God my desires and praise. He makes it possible for me to speak to God with wisdom.

In the same way, the Spirit helps us in our weakness. We do not know how we ought to pray, but the Spirit himself intercedes for us with groans that words cannot express (Rom. 8:26 NIV).

Dear Jesus, thank You for Your Holy Spirit who intercedes for me and knows how to pray when I don't. Amen.

COMPLETE TRUST

Much is said in the Bible about Paul of Tarsus, before and after his conversion. But it's easy to overlook Ananias, the man whose faith was needed to save Paul.

When Ananias was sent to talk to Paul about God, Paul was a dangerous man, with authority to arrest Christians. In spite of these dangers, Ananias put his trust completely in God and obeyed Him. Because of this, God was able to do a great thing through him. His example is an inspiring one, showing me how much God can do when I trust Him completely.

In Damascus there was a disciple named Ananias. The Lord called to him in a vision, "Ananias!" "Yes, Lord," he answered (Acts 9:10 NIV).

Thank You, God, for examples of men of great faith like Ananias. Help me to have more faith. Amen.

October 16

NO DISAGREEMENT

I listened as two people talked to each other. They were growing quite upset because, to each of them, the other seemed to be stubborn and rude. Hearing both sides, I soon realized that neither was hearing correctly what the other was saying. When I asked each what he was hearing the other person say, they laughed at themselves. The mis-understanding had come from the smaller misunderstand-ing of each individual. When each knew what the other had really said, there was no more disagreement.

That situation made me wonder how often I become upset with people merely because I don't hear what they're really saying. Maybe if I'd be more careful to listen well, many disagreements would disappear.

> **Do not judge, and you will not be judged. Do not condemn, and you will not be condemned. Forgive, and you will be forgiven (Luke 6:37 NIV).**

Lord, guide me through each day and each conversation. I pray that I will try to understand others rather than being quick to judge them. Amen.

October 17

JOY OF LIVING

I have a friend who always looks happy. She seems to enjoy every moment of life and makes experiences that would be boring for others, fresh with excitement. As we became closer friends, I realized that she was an ordinary person, with extraordinary faith.

With Jesus, it is possible to make every day an exciting adventure. I am challenged by each experience, to show my faith through the joy of living.

> **So I say to you: Ask and it will be given to you; seek and you will find; knock and the door will be opened to you (Luke 11:9 NIV).**

Father, teach me to respond to everyday experiences with a fresh attitude. Thank You for providing a reason to be joyful. Amen.

A HALF-BAKED LIFE

Trying a new recipe for a cake turned into a disaster. After it was baked and cooled, it looked good, but when it was cut open, it lost its attraction. The inside was a mass of heavy, soggy dough. I hadn't baked it long enough.

Unless I live according to God's direction each day, I am not fully ready to serve the purpose He has for me. What it looks like on the outside isn't necessarily what it is on the inside until He has total control over me.

My people mingle with the heathen, picking up their evil ways; thus they become as good-for-nothing as a half-baked cake! (Hos. 7:8 LB).

Lord, help me to "bake" evenly so the inside is as good as the outside looks. Thank You for living in me. Amen.

STRENGTH TO PEDAL

Riding my bicycle through the hills around my home has provided many hours of enjoyment. The hard work of pedaling up the hills is rewarded by the fun of flying downhill with little effort. When I reach the bottom, however, I must begin with renewed energy to tackle the next climb. If I coast until the bike slows down, it's harder to regain momentum.

When life is easy, I sometimes forget that hard times may lie ahead. I should be ready to start with renewed strength so I have enough energy to get me to the top. God gives me assurance that He will help me up the next hill too.

You need to persevere so that when you have done the will of God, you will receive what he has promised (Heb. 10:36 NIV).

Thank You, God, for helping me gain momentum on the "down-hills" of life to help me up the next climb. Give me strength when the hill becomes long and hard. Amen.

October 20

THE PSALM OF THE GOOD TEACHER

The Lord is my Teacher;
I shall not lose the way to wisdom.
He leadeth me in the lowly path of learning,
He prepareth a lesson for me every day.
He findeth the clear fountain of instruction —
Little by little He showeth me the beauty of truth.
The world is a great book that He has written,
He turneth the leaves for me slowly;
They are all inscribed with images and letters —
His voice poureth light on the pictures and the words.
Then am I glad when I perceive His meaning.
He taketh me by the hand to the hilltop of wisdom;
In the valley, also, He walketh beside me,
And in the dark places He whispereth in my heart.
Yea, though my lesson be hard, it is not hopeless,
For the Lord is very patient with His slow scholar.
He will wait for my weakness —
He will help me to read the truth through tears —
Surely Thou wilt enlighten me daily by joy and by
    sorrow,
And lead me at last, O Lord, to the perfect knowledge
    of Thee.

— Henry van Dyke

Because the Lord is my Shepherd, I have everything I need! (Ps. 23:1 LB).

Thank You for being my Teacher and Lord. I give the difficulty of my lessons over to You. Please help me with them. Amen.

PASS IT ON

I have a friend who loves to do things for other people, and she doesn't expect anything in return. When it's impossible for me to repay her acts of kindness, she tells me to do something for someone else, and that will be pay enough.

She is a beautiful example of the kind of love Christ has for me. I can never repay Him for what He's done for me, but I can show my gratitude by spreading His love to others.

Jesus told him, "Go and do likewise" (Luke 10:37 NIV).

Your love, Jesus, is more than I can repay except by telling others about it. Thank You for Your amazing love. Amen.

MIGHTY GOD

When I reached the top of a mountain with a group of friends, we broke into songs of praise to God. The view was beautiful as we looked down on miles of trees and up into the clear blue sky. Seeing the earth from high above, as God does, made us feel especially close to Him.

By seeing all the beauty and majesty in God's creation, I saw myself as only a tiny part of His vast purpose on earth. I felt the great privilege of having God, who made all that I saw, as my personal Savior.

**My help is from Jehovah who made the mountains!
And the heavens too! (Ps. 121:2 LB).**

*O mighty Savior, I praise You for caring about me amidst all
the grandeur of Your creation. Thank You for the beauty all
around me. Amen.*

COMMUNICATION TECHNIQUES

Words cannot only make a friendship, but they can also
break it. For this reason, God gives rules for their use,
found in the Book of James.

Listening takes time, but when love listens, the time is
well spent. Too often I don't listen enough but speak too
much. Unwise words can be a powerful tool of destruction.
They may lead to anger, which can do great damage. I must
be more considerate in communicating to others through
my words and times of listening.

**My dear brothers, take note of this: Everyone should
be quick to listen, slow to speak, and slow to become
angry (James 1:19 NIV).**

*Teach me, O God, to be more sensitive to others in my words,
silences, and actions. Thank You for being patient with me
when I fail. Amen.*

October 24

UNRECOGNIZED HONOR

Often it's hardest to see good things in people I've known
the longest. I think I know them so well that I no longer try
to see new actions or talents they may have.

Jesus is a good example. Though He was the Son of God

and did many miracles, the people of Nazareth didn't accept Him. Knowing His earthly parents, they couldn't believe He was greater than anyone else.

I must look at those I know in a new light every day. Only then can I see their abilities as God sees them.

Jesus said to them, "Only in his home town, among his relatives and in his own house is a prophet without honor" (Mark 6:4 NIV).

Prevent me, Lord, from failing to see the virtues of those near me. Help me to always look for the good in others. Amen.

October 25

THE DIFFICULTY OF SELF-FORGIVENESS

From a recent experience, I've discovered that sometimes it's harder to forgive myself than for the person I've wronged to forgive me. When I tried to play a joke on a friend, it turned out to be a painful experience for him. After talking to him about it, he forgave me, but the stupidity of my thoughtlessness bothered me for days.

God said He will take our sins so far away we can never find them again. With this promise, I shouldn't let guilt haunt my mind after I've been forgiven. I must learn to forgive myself because God has and go on from there.

He has removed our sins as far away from us as the east is from the west (Ps. 103:12 LB).

Thank You, God, for Your forgiving Spirit. Teach me to forgive myself too. Amen.

October 26

KNOW THE WORK

Lured by the glory football players receive after a good game, one of my friends decided to join the team one year.

After a week of hard practice he quit. He hadn't realized how tough the work was.

The same thing can happen in my life if I look at the gloriousness of life in Christ and miss the hardships. Jesus makes it clear that His way isn't the easiest. I shouldn't let my enthusiasm block out the cost of discipleship, but always be willing to be a hard worker.

> **As they were walking along the road, a man said to him, "I will follow you wherever you go." Jesus replied, "Foxes have holes and birds of the air have nests, but the Son of Man has no place to lay his head" (Luke 9:57,58 NIV).**

Your way, O Lord, may not be the easiest, but it is the most worthwhile. I want to continue following You. Amen.

October 27

GOD SHINES THROUGH

The sun comes up every morning whether I notice it or not. It provides light for me and makes my food grow even if I don't always appreciate it.

Like the sun, God shines into my life each day, just like He shines over the whole world. It's up to me to make sure I don't become too busy to notice or appreciate His light and warmth shining on me and on all the rest of His creation.

> **Let everything he has made give praise to him (Ps. 148:5 LB).**

Almighty Father, grant that I will never take Your shining love for granted, but that I may look anew each day at the great privilege of knowing You. Amen.

JESUS AS THE GUIDE

One day dad was driving along a highway behind a truck. As the truck turned off onto a side road, dad followed. By the time he realized his mistake, a whole string of cars were following him too.

It's easy to be led astray by others without giving it much thought. Jesus came into the world to save those who are lost and to lead them back to the right way. I must continually look to Him to show me the way and not be distracted by the direction others take.

And I, the Messiah, came to save the lost (Matt. 18:11 LB).

Thank You, Jesus, for showing me the way. Prevent me from following others merely because they seem to be going the way I'm going. Amen.

FREE FROM SIN

After a heavy rain, my brother and I went for a walk. When we came to a bank that was covered with mud, my brother slid down it. It looked like fun and I couldn't resist. When I slid down, however, I fell, twisted my arm, and pulled a muscle. Seeing only the pleasure, I hadn't anticipated the pain that followed.

Sinful ways sometimes look attractive too. They don't look harmful at first, but if I yield, unexpected results may take place. Christ knows the deceitful ways of sin and wants to set me free from sin's trap. By following Him, I no longer fall captive to the bonds of sin.

You have been set free from sin and have become slaves to righteousness (Rom. 6:18 NIV).

Thank You, Lord, for freeing me from sin and its cunning ways of deception. Guide me in the way of righteousness. Amen.

GOD IS

Is it possible to believe there is no God? I don't see how. In the words of Nikita Ivanovich Panin, "The world we inhabit must have had an origin; that origin must have consisted in a cause; that cause must have been intelligent; that intelligence must have been supreme; and that supreme, which always was and is supreme, we know by the name of God."

One God and Father of all, who is over all and through all and in all (Eph. 4:6 NIV).

Thank You, God, for Your supreme intelligence that caused the origin of the world. I will praise Your name forever. Amen.

CLOSENESS COUNTS

From the many tours I've been on, I know the importance of staying near the guide. When I wander off by myself or lag behind, I miss all the facts the guide is relating.

When I wander after my own desires and interests, I can no longer hear what Jesus is saying and I become frustrated. Only by staying as near to His leading as possible can I be sure I'm hearing all that He says to me.

If you will only let me help you, if you will only obey, then I will make you rich! (Isa. 1:19 LB).

Father, thank You for being the Guide of my life. Grant that I will always stay close enough to hear You. Amen.

ENJOYING LAZINESS

An article entitled "How to Be Lazy — and Love It" caught my attention. I don't usually have a problem being lazy, but when I do it's hard to enjoy it without feeling guilty. I was amused and helped by the following suggestions:

Be too lazy to frown, fidget, or fuss.
Listen more than you talk.
Don't bother quarreling over insignificant things.
Don't knock yourself out for a bargain that takes more out of you than it saves the piggy bank.
Be too lazy to worry your mind with the inevitable.

This is the best way I have found to be lazy and love it. Those close to me also enjoy this kind of laziness in me.

O Israel, you too should quietly trust in the Lord — now, and always (Ps. 131:3 LB).

Thank You, Lord, for these directions for being lazy. Help me put them into practice. Amen.

NOTHING CAN BE HIDDEN

Cleaning my room for a friend's visit, I didn't have time to put everything away, so I threw some things under the bed. They were out of sight, but not out of my mind. Later, I took them out and put them where they belonged.

This incident made me think of how I sometimes try to block things out of my mind — hurting others, a cutting remark, or my insensitivity to someone's needs. I may be able to hide my wrong for awhile, but it will never disappear completely until I make it right.

There is nothing concealed that will not be disclosed, or hidden that will not be made known (Matt. 10:26 NIV).

Forgive me, Father, for times when I've tried to ignore things I've done wrong. Thank You for helping me to see the necessity of correcting them. Amen.

November 3

HANG ON

I heard the story of a girl who dreamed that she died and went to heaven. Seeing her name on a box in the corner marked "Prayer Requests," she asked an angel what it was. The angel said that when God's children make a request, the answer is prepared, but if the petitioner is not waiting for it, it is returned and stored in this corner.

Waiting is difficult, but it is not in vain if we wait expectantly and patiently. An old proverb says, "When you come to the end of your rope, tie a prayer knot and hang on."

But if we hope for what we do not yet have, we wait for it patiently (Rom. 8:25 NIV).

Lord, grant that I will have expectancy for an answer to my prayers and the patience to hang on and wait. Amen.

November 4

DIFFERENT FORMATIONS

A lump of dirty, black coal and a beautiful, glimmering diamond don't seem to have many similarities, but both are composed of nearly the same elements. The difference is in the way they were formed.

People are quite different from one another, too, although basically the same. God made each person in His own image. The difference is in the formation. When I give my life to Christ, He molds me into a new person. Instead of thinking bad things of other people, I should remember that the only difference between us is in the way we were formed.

Men judge by outward appearance, but I look at a man's thoughts and intentions (1 Sam. 16:7 LB).

Thank You, God, for forming my life. I want to continually give myself to You for Your molding. Amen.

November 5

SLOW DOWN

"Take it easy. Slow down. Think about what you're doing." Those were familiar words from our basketball coach when we became tense in a game and made careless mistakes.

It's good advice for the rest of life as well. God wants me to put forth my best efforts, but at the same time, slow down enough to do things right. He has the rhythm for my life planned. My job is to learn that rhythm and live within it with God as my coach.

He will keep in perfect peace all those who trust in him, whose thoughts turn often to the Lord! (Isa. 26:3 LB).

Thank You, Master, for coaching my game of life. If I forget Your advice and step out of Your timing, tell me to slow down. Amen.

SPIRITUAL STRENGTH

Doctors say that most people don't use their full physical strength. Several stories exist, however, of people who possess extra strength in emergencies, such as lifting a car to save a person's life. Further, psychologists say that only a fraction of our mental abilities is ever used.

The same is probably true of spiritual powers. If I were warned about each experience before it happened, I might not think I have enough strength to handle it. But each time, God provides enough power. I must rely on Him to give me strength to face every situation.

I pray also that the eyes of your heart may be enlightened in order that you may know the hope to which he has called you, the riches of his glorious inheritance in the saints, and his incomparably great power for us who believe (Eph. 1:18,19 NIV).

Thank You, God, for giving me Your special strength in every situation we face together. Continue to be my guide. Amen.

LOOK AHEAD

When I shop with my mother she tells me that after I buy something, I shouldn't look at the same thing in another store. I might have made the worst bargain but it's too late to change, so I'll feel better by not comparing.

The same principle is true throughout life. Continually comparing the present to the past, wishing I had done something different, brings discontentment. The only thing I have control over is what I do now. Worrying about the past doesn't change anything. By giving my past failures to God, I can go on with a lighter load.

But one thing I do: Forgetting what is behind and straining toward what is ahead (Phil. 3:13 NIV).

Heavenly Father, help me to look ahead and do what I can instead of regretting the past that I can't change. Thank You for loving me in spite of all my past failures. Amen.

November 8

COURTESY

An unknown author wrote, "I am a little thing with a big meaning. I help unlock doors, open hearts, and dispel prejudice. I create friendships and good will. I inspire respect and admiration. Everybody loves me. I bore nobody. I violate no law. I cost nothing. Many have praised me; no one has condemned me. I am useful every moment of the day in many ways. I am called courtesy."

Finally, all of you, live in harmony with one another; be sympathetic, love as brothers, be compassionate and humble (1 Peter 3:8 NIV).

Lord, help me to be courteous to everyone I come in contact with. Thank You for Your example of courtesy. Amen.

November 9

MEANING OF DISCIPLESHIP

In Greek, the word for *disciple* means "learner" and carries with it the idea of discipline. Jesus, however, uses it with a much deeper meaning. He taught the need for total commitment of one's life to His authority if one would be

His disciple. I can only be a true disciple of Jesus when I'm willing to put my own desires aside for His will.

To the Jews who had believed him, Jesus said, "If you hold to my teaching, you are really my disciples" (John 8:31 NIV).

Thank You, Jesus, that it is possible to be Your disciple. Guide me in everything I do that I will remain under Your authority. Amen.

UNKNOWN WATERS

A friend and I were canoeing down a river when we decided to stop and hike on land for awhile. Upon returning to the place where we had tied our canoe, we found that some friends had taken it to the other side as a joke! We were helpless without it, so we started across. We found, too late, that what looked like a beautiful, peaceful river from the shore, had a strong, turbulent current beneath the surface that threatened to pull us under. With a struggle and a prayer, we eventually made it to the other side.

That river reminds me of some things in life. From a distance, they look safe, but when I become involved, the opposite is true. If I learn to pray before I venture into unknown waters, many extra struggles can be eliminated.

Humble yourselves, therefore, under God's mighty hand, that he may lift you up in due time (1 Peter 5:6 NIV).

Thank You, Father, for helping me out of troubled waters I sometimes become caught in. Guide me in the future to be more careful of what I step into. Amen.

WORK AT LOVE

Many think of love as a beautiful relationship which suddenly springs forth. Like a storybook romance, things fall together and a couple lives happily ever after. But like a flower that blooms only after much cultivation and care, love also takes work. Instead of *falling* in love, I must *grow* in love.

In the same way, following Jesus with a deep, increasing expression of His love does not just happen. I must work at becoming His disciple. I must follow Him day by day to learn how to love Him more and share His love with others.

Then he said to them all: "If anyone would come after me, he must deny himself and take up his cross daily and follow me (Luke 9:23 NIV).

Give me patience, Lord, to work at becoming Your disciple just as I must work at everything else that's worthwhile. Amen.

TAKE A CLOSER LOOK

One day in a science class, we looked at flowers under a microscope. The beauty of each intricate part of what had previously been an ordinary looking flower was impossible to describe. Each person had to look himself to experience the joy. Since then I have recognized more beauty in each flower I see, because I know more of what's there.

Jesus, in His glory, is that way too. Each person must take the time to discover for himself Jesus' true beauty. No words can do justice to the real picture of what life with Him is like. Once His glory has been seen, the only regret is that it wasn't known before.

The Word became flesh and lived for a while among us. We have seen his glory, the glory of the one and only Son, who came from the Father, full of grace and truth (John 1:14 NIV).

Thank You, Jesus, for making Yourself available for everyone to see. Grant that I will help encourage others to discover Your true beauty also. Amen.

November 13

LIFE — A BOOK

In an article "If I Were 17 Again . . . and Know What I Know at 80," Josephine Fox Fink writes: "At 17 life is like a beautiful book in a gorgeous binding, but with blank pages you fill in from day to day in your life. I would try to live so that there would be no pages that I would want to skip over or tear out. Others would be pages to laugh about when I recalled them, and of course there would be sad pages, but they would be few and far between."

I like that. I like to think of life as a book of empty pages and that God has created me to choose what will be printed on those pages. It is a great privilege and responsibility — one I cannot fulfill alone.

You alone are my God; my times are in your hands (Ps. 31:14,15 LB).

God, thank You for life and that You promised to be with me, to enable me to choose and do what makes life beautiful. Amen.

November 14

ANGELS TODAY

A friend and I were standing at the top of a hill one evening, looking over the lights below. Suddenly, a man walked out from the shadows and began talking to us. He said that many of the people around that hill don't know Jesus, but those who do know Him don't seem to have time to share Him. Therefore many would continue to live in darkness.

When he descended again into the shadows, we felt we had been visited by one of God's angels. Even though our visitor didn't look any different from us, we felt God had sent him to deliver that message. I must always be listening for God's voice no matter how He sends it.

> **As they talked and discussed these things with each other, Jesus himself came up and walked along with them; but they were kept from recognizing him (Luke 24:15,16 NIV).**

Thank You, Father, for sending angels today too. May I always be listening for what You are saying to me through Your messengers. Amen.

November 15

A LITTLE AT A TIME

"The best way to get much done is to always be doing a little." Those were the words on a plaque at school. I thought about them when the amount of work to be done seemed so huge that I hardly knew where to start. I learned that the best way to deal with that is to start somewhere and not think about the rest until there's time to do it. Surprisingly enough, things get done faster that way than when I worry about them. Thinking only of what I'm doing makes that project more enjoyable than if I only think of it in the context of all that remains to be done.

> **Therefore do not worry about tomorrow, for tomorrow will worry about itself. Each day has enough trouble of its own (Matt. 6:34 NIV).**

Thank You for helping me get things done, Lord, and for the knowledge that I don't need to spend time worrying about them. Amen.

POINTING BACK AT ME

As a child, when questioned about some wrongdoing, it wasn't unusual for me to point at one of my brothers or sister, trying to replace the blame. It also wasn't unusual for one of them to say, "You have three fingers pointing back at yourself." I didn't like that reminder, but it was true.

Today when I point at others who do wrong, it's still true that I have three fingers pointing back at myself. After all the times God has forgiven me, how can I point at others for doing wrong? I can only ask God to forgive me.

When they kept on questioning him, he straightened up and said to them, "If any one of you is without sin, let him begin stoning her" (John 8:7 NIV).

Forgive me, God, for pointing my finger too often and blaming others. Give me the strength to take my own responsibility. Amen.

November 17

TAKE MY LIFE

Take my life and let it be
Consecrated, Lord, to Thee;
Take my moments and my days:
Let them flow in ceaseless praise.

This song has deep meaning when I pray it sincerely from my heart as well as sing it with my mouth. I'm saying that every moment of every day is God's to use as He wills, and I will continue to praise Him. And why shouldn't I? He bought me with a high price. By accepting Him as my Lord, I consecrate my life to Him.

You are not your own; you were bought at a price. Therefore honor God with your body (1 Cor. 6:19,20 NIV).

My life, O Lord, is in Your hands. Thank You for the joy of serving You. Amen.

November 18

SERENDIPITY

The word *serendipity* means to discover something good by accident. It comes from a story about the King of Serendip, who sent his sons on a journey. Since they were obedient and faithful, they discovered beautiful and valuable treasures all along the way.

My main goal today is to find the will of God and do it; but all along the way, He plants exciting surprises in my path. I cannot foresee all that God has in store for me. I can only praise Him for what He continually provides.

But seek first his kingdom and his righteousness, and all these things will be given to you as well (Matt. 6:33 NIV).

Thank You, heavenly King, for all the unexpected joy and happiness You've given me. Amen.

November 19

BOUGHT TWICE

At the end of each school year, an afternoon is set aside to give the students an opportunity to buy what has accumulated in the lost-and-found box. After an item is on the auctioning table, it's too late to claim it as lost. One of my friends recognized one of her shirts among the items and bought it back.

It didn't seem fair that she had to pay for the shirt twice. Neither does it seem fair that God had to pay twice for each one of His children — but He did. I belong to Him first because He created me, and second because He bought me with the blood of His Son.

For you know that it was not with perishable things such as silver or gold that you were redeemed from the empty way of life handed down to you from your forefathers, but with the precious blood of Christ (1 Peter 1:18,19 NIV).

Thank You, Jesus, for Your love that was great enough to make me Yours twice. Amen.

November 20

STAY ALERT

The father of one of my friends is a volunteer fireman and policeman. They have an instrument in their home which announces any need for help. It stays on all the time, and as soon as help is called for, no matter what he's doing, he goes. He fully participates in all the activities at home, but he also keeps his ears open for any emergency directions.

As a follower of Jesus, I must have the same kind of built-in alertness and loyalty. In my activities every day, I need to be constantly receptive to any directions the Holy Spirit sends me and be willing to act accordingly.

Those who are led by the Spirit of God are sons of God (Rom. 8:14 NIV).

Thank You, God, for Your Spirit to give me directions for my life. Thank You for the desire to do Your will. Grant that I will remain alert for Your call. Amen.

IMPRISONED

With no jail near our house, I wondered how I could fulfill Christ's command to visit those in prison. I had read about prison conditions, but had never been inside one.

Then I began to think about other kinds of prisons people are in — imprisoned by fears, insecurity, hate, wealth, or stubbornness. Bars and keys aren't the only things that bind people. Jesus came to release the captives of these prisons. As His messenger, I am to visit them to tell of His help. Jesus said that whatever I do for the least of these, it is as if I've done it for Him.

I was in prison and you came to visit me (Matt. 25:36 NIV).

Guide me, Lord, in doing Your work – sharing with those who have become imprisoned by the miseries of life. Help me to know how to be a friend to them. Amen.

LIVING FOR OTHERS

When my brother returned from visiting friends, he brought a recipe with him for homemade bread. He liked it so well that he wanted to learn to make it himself. His first loaves weren't as good as those his friends had made, but he kept trying, and each time they turned out better. Soon our family thought his bread was better than any other kind.

Doing good deeds is like baking bread. The more often I do them, the easier they become. When it becomes natural to do things for others, I can no longer be satisfied with living only for myself.

> **He who has been stealing must steal no longer, but must work, doing something useful with his own hands, that he may have something to share with those in need (Eph. 4:28 NIV).**

Thank You, Father, for the desire to do good deeds. Make them so much a part of my life that I would be uncomfortable not doing them. Amen.

November 23

A PILE OF ASHES

It was late in the fall when I went camping with a group of friends. The only heat in our cabin was a fireplace. Before we went to bed, we built a big fire, which hopefully was to last all night. But in the morning, all that remained was a pile of ashes. By blowing on the hot ashes and putting small shavings of wood and pieces of paper on them, the fire was soon rekindled.

Jesus probably sees my life as a pile of ashes sometimes. In the ashes of coming to the end of my own resources, He breathes new life into me and rekindles my flame. My fire must not only last until the next morning, but for all eternity.

> **Then Abraham spoke again. "Since I have begun, let me go on and speak further to the Lord, though I am but dust and ashes" (Gen. 18:27 LB).**

Thank You, Jesus, for the breath of Your Spirit blowing in me. Grant that my flame will always be kindled for Your ministry. Amen.

GIVE THANKS

At our Thanksgiving dinner, each of us found five kernels of corn on our plate. Before we began the meal, we were each to think of five things we were thankful for. I kept those kernels on my desk for a long time to remind myself of all that I have to be thankful for.

Thanksgiving isn't the only day to think of the many blessings God has given me. Maybe this year I should take an entire corncob and think of something for each kernel. I'm sure I wouldn't run out of things I can thank Him for.

I will praise the Lord and call on all men everywhere to bless his holy name forever and forever (Ps. 145:21 LB).

Thank You, God, for the many things You have given me to be thankful for. I will praise Your name forever. Amen.

RUN THE RACE

As I watched the Olympics on television, I was awed by the power, strength, and endurance, not only of the winners, but of each participant. Pictures were shown of their hours of training and hard work that preceded the competitions. The ones who received no recognition had been faithful in the difficult times just as those who received medals.

God has a prize for each one who perseveres in running His race. Recognition for being the best runner isn't as important as the faithfulness to continue the race.

I have fought the good fight, I have finished the race, I have kept the faith (2 Tim. 4:7 NIV).

Creator, give me strength and perseverence to do Your will today. Help me to endure to the end. Amen.

ACTIVE GOOD WILL

"I don't love him any more. I'm filing for a divorce." "I don't love my parents. I'm going to live with someone else." These words have become too common in the world today. The word *love* has so many different meanings, it can be confusing.

The meaning of *love* as Paul uses it in Ephesians, however, is different than a love based merely on feelings. It means "active good will." With God's help and my desire, I can exercise this kind of love. Christian love is lasting and stable.

And live a life of love, just as Christ loved us and gave himself up for us as a fragrant offering and sacrifice to God (Eph. 5:2 NIV).

O God, help me to exercise active good will and not base my love merely on good feelings. Thank You for Your continual love. Amen.

FROM BAD TO BEAUTIFUL

A friend of mine once wrote a beautiful song, using the tune of a song which originally had offensive words. Even though the tune was the same, he had completely changed the meaning of the song.

It reminds me of some of the bad times I have experienced. Depending on what I do with them, they may have good or bad consequences. Like the tune of a song, events may not be bad in themselves, but how I handle them determines how they turn out. My responsibility as a follower of Christ is to do my best to make the most out of rough situations. He can bring about tremendous change.

For the Son of Man came to seek and to save what was lost (Luke 19:10 NIV).

Father, thank You for coming to make good out of the bad. Thank You for working in me. Amen.

November 28

COVER-UP

A layer of newly fallen snow is a beautiful sight to wake up to in the morning. All the dirt and trash are covered with a blanket of white. When it begins to melt, however, the filth is seen again.

Sometimes I try to hide the trash in my life by looking good on the outside. I may be successful for awhile in the eyes of those around me, but I can't fool God. When He takes away all that is false at the final judgment, my true nature will be visible. I must live so that nothing is covered.

Not everyone who says to me, "Lord, Lord," will enter the kingdom of heaven, but only he who does the will of my Father who is in heaven (Matt. 7:21 NIV).

Make me pure, O God, so that I won't be ashamed when every part of me is uncovered. Guide me in following Your will. Amen.

November 29

IN THE NOISE

Some days it seems impossible to escape the noise long enough to talk to God for awhile. When I'm finally alone in the quiet of my room, the phone rings, someone needs help, or the neighbors start making noise.

In loud and busy situations, it's more difficult to feel God's presence than when it's quiet and peaceful. It takes more faith to know He's with me when I can't hear His voice as clearly. But I can't forget that He is still near. Whether it's noisy or quiet, God is waiting for me.

And surely I will be with you always, to the very end of the age (Matt. 28:20 NIV).

Dear Lord, help me to remember You when I'm struggling with outside influences. Thank You that my faith doesn't need to depend on circumstances. Amen.

November 30

HELD BY GOD

As the airplane flew higher into the sky, the fields, buildings, and roads became smaller. Soon white clouds surrounded the plane and nothing else was visible.

It was the first time I had ever been in the clouds, and I felt a beautiful closeness to God. I could see nothing except the airplane which kept me up, but that was all that was necessary. It helped me to see that the only thing that matters in my life is the faith in God which holds me up. All my little problems are insignificant when I'm surrounded by God's love and the light of His presence.

When Jesus spoke again to the people, he said, "I am the light of the world. Whoever follows me will never walk in darkness, but will have the light of life" (John 8:12 NIV).

Thank You, Jesus, for giving me the light of life. Guide me in the ways You lead. Amen.

December 1

JESUS UNDERSTANDS

A friend told me that her dog became frightened when his stomach growled. Unaware that it was coming from his own stomach, he was frustrated when he couldn't escape the noise.

It sounds funny, but I wonder how many times I'm like that. Sometimes I become uneasy about my feelings, not knowing why I have them nor how to stop them. Then I remember that Jesus was once a human too and had the same feelings. He understands my feelings before I've experienced them and is always ready to help me deal with them. It's a privilege to have a protector who understands me and is willing to help me understand myself.

Praise be to the God and Father of our Lord Jesus Christ, the Father of compassion and the God of all comfort (2 Cor. 1:3 NIV).

Thank You, Lord, for being with me when I don't understand my own feelings. Help me to accept what I can't understand without letting it hinder the rest of my life. Amen.

December 2

TRANSFORMING POWER

The talent of artists has always fascinated me. The way they transform simple tools, such as paper, pencils, paint, and canvas, into pieces of beauty is amazing.

Yet more amazing than any creation by a human artist is the transforming power of Christ. He can change what looks small and worthless into something of eternal value. One life, transformed by His hands, is more valuable than any piece of art a man can produce.

Do not conform any longer to the pattern of this world, but be transformed by the renewing of your mind (Rom. 12:2 NIV).

Your power, O Christ, of transforming lives is incredible. I invite You to make the worthless, unattractive parts of me into something beautiful. Thank You. Amen.

December 3

ACCEPTING FORGIVENESS

Every meaningful relationship involves a dialogue. Each person must give and take with the other.

To have a meaningful relationship with God, I must give myself to Him and also accept what He offers me. Man is the only part of God's creation that has the privilege of His companionship. Our fellowship was broken by sin, but Christ died to restore it. My part in our relationship is to accept His forgiveness.

I am ready to make an everlasting covenant with you, to give you all the unfailing mercies and love that I had for King David (Isa. 55:3 LB).

Teach me, God, to accept Your forgiveness with gratefulness. Help me to guard against breaking our communication by my refusal to give or take. Thank You for the relationship I can have with You. Amen.

December 4

CHRIST MUST BE FIRST

By holding a pencil in front of my eye, I can block a window out of my view. By holding it closer, I can block out an entire house. It doesn't seem possible for something so small to block out a much larger object; but when each is in the right place, it can be done easily.

So it is with Christ. He is incomprehensibly large, but if I allow something to come between us, no matter how small, it can block Him out. Pride, money, possessions, or anything I hold dearer than Christ, diminishes my view of Him. I must be careful to put Christ first and put everything else behind Him.

He is before all things, and in him all things hold together (Col. 1:17 NIV).

Grant, O Lord, that I will not allow anything to come between us and hinder my view of You. Thank You for Your help. Amen.

December 5

CHRISTIANS IN ACTION

"Do not disturb the peace" — every citizen knows these words must be obeyed to stay out of trouble with the authorities. The law is good, but many seem to have adopted it into their spiritual lives too. Often new ideas are squelched and nothing is done that will upset the status quo.

Jesus and His disciples came to turn the world upside down. They didn't teach only the things they knew would be accepted, but they spoke and lived the truth, taking the risk of being called troublemakers. I too must refuse to be content if something contradicts what I know is right in my life with Christ.

These men who have caused trouble all over the world have now come here (Acts 17:6 NIV).

Give me guidance, Lord, to know when to speak out for You. Thank You for Your example of standing up for what is right. Amen.

CUT OFF FROM GOD

As a joke, I sent a letter to my friend without signing my name. After she received it, I avoided her for the rest of the day, afraid I couldn't act normal around her and that she would figure out that I had sent it.

I did that for fun, but it's not fun when my sins cut me off from fellowship with God. If I do something wrong, I must ask Him for forgiveness before our relationship can be restored. I must confess my sins before walls have a chance to grow between us.

> **But the trouble is that your sins have cut you off from God (Isa. 59:2 LB).**

Heavenly Father, forgive me when I allow my sins to cut me off from You. Thank You for Your patience with me and Your total acceptance. Amen.

December 7

THE OPEN LINE

As I made the third attempt to place a long-distance phone call to a friend, I hoped a line would be open this time so I could get through. I was relieved to hear the phone ring and finally the voice of my friend on the other end.

It's comforting to know that a line exists between God and me that is never too busy or overloaded for my call to get through — the channel of prayer. Even if everyone were talking to God, my call would go through and I could communicate with Him. If the line of prayer is not in use, the fault can only be my own. God is always waiting with an open line.

For the Lord says, . . . "When he calls on me I will answer; I will be with him in trouble, and rescue him and honor him" (Ps. 91:14,15 LB).

Thank You, Father, that the line to You is always open. Help me to remember to keep the communication open. Amen.

THANK GOD — NO FLIES

Last winter the thought suddenly hit me that all the flies were hibernating for the winter, and none were flying around being pesky. . . .! I always knew they only came out in the summer, but I didn't really think about how nice it is not to have them around in the winter.

In the summer I do my share of complaining about flies when they're bothersome, but when they leave, I don't think about praising God for their absence. It reminds me of how much I complain about things instead of praising God for the pleasures I do have.

And be thankful (Col. 3:15 NIV).

Thank You, God, that the pesky flies aren't around in the winter. Help me to look for things to praise You for instead of complaining. Amen.

HE'S ALWAYS WATCHING

When my sister and I were young, we loved to jump on our bed. We knew we weren't allowed to do it, but when no one was in the house, we sometimes sneaked up to our room to jump anyway. We thought we were safe as long as no one caught us. Then one day the bed broke, and we were forced to admit the wrong we had done.

Sometimes I'm tempted to think that other things I do won't matter either, as long as no one sees me. But unlike my parents, God is always watching me. I must live every minute the way I want Him to see me.

Live as children of light (for the fruit of the light consists in all goodness, righteousness and truth) (Eph. 5:8,9 NIV).

I appreciate Your constant watching, Lord. Keep me from anything You don't approve of. Amen.

December 10

INTERTWINING FOR SUPPORT

The great redwood trees in California have always fascinated me, even though I've seen them only in pictures. Some of them are 300 feet high and 2,500 years old! Since most trees have a root system that is as deep as the tree is tall, a redwood's root system could be expected to be vast, but that isn't true. It has a shallow root system. The secret of its survival is its dependence on other redwood trees. They grow in groves, so that their roots intertwine and support each other.

I often think of the greatest as being the most independent, but as the redwood trees proved, to be great requires support from others. I shouldn't be too proud to admit my need of others. By intertwining my life with other people, I can be stronger than if I try to stand alone.

So in Christ we who are many form one body, and each member belongs to all the others (Rom. 12:5 NIV).

Thank You, Lord, for the friends You've given me to intertwine my life with for maximum support and strength. Amen.

FREEDOM IN CHRIST

I had a classmate who became an alcoholic. He began to drink in high school as a way of expressing his freedom from authority. But the means by which he sought freedom became exactly what later enslaved him. His body was a slave to the need of drink.

Evil seems to promise freedom, but if I yield to it, my soul becomes stifled and imprisoned. Christ alone provides real freedom. When I turn each day over to Him, I have freedom that cannot be found through any other means.

Restore to me again the joy of your salvation, and make me willing to obey you (Ps. 51:12 LB).

Jesus Christ, I thank You for the freedom You've given me. Grant that I will only seek freedom in Your will. Amen.

HUMAN WORTH

Each year as I hear about the large number of people killed in accidents on the highways, I am momentarily sad. It was not until one of my friends was killed, however, that I experienced the real sorrow that each death causes.

Jesus had compassion for all people because He knew the worth of each one.

He came into the world to save every person, and He is grieved with each soul that is lost. The way to show my love for Jesus is to show compassion for everyone, just as He did.

In the same way your Father in heaven is not willing that any of these little ones should be lost (Matt. 18:14 NIV).

Eternal God, forgive me for times I haven't cared enough about my fellow human beings. Thank You for Your example of compassion. Amen.

WAIT UPON THE LORD

Waiting isn't easy. Everyone can testify to that from personal experiences, like waiting for a date to arrive, waiting for Christmas, waiting for a wound to heal, or waiting for the day a loved one will be seen again. These and many others are common situations people find themselves in — situations that sometimes seem unbearable.

For those who wait upon the Lord, however, He promises renewed strength. God will never faint or grow weary, and He offers power to those who trust Him. When I learn to wait on God, I will no longer grow weary. He will help me to endure any trial or hardship.

> **But they that wait upon the Lord shall renew their strength. They shall mount up with wings like eagles; they shall run and not be weary; they shall walk and not faint (Isa. 40:31 LB).**

Teach me, Lord, to wait upon You for all my needs. Give me patience as I wait. Amen.

INDIVIDUALITY

An interesting place our family sometimes stops to visit has bushes all over the yard. Each bush has been trimmed into the shape of a different animal. The bushes, which were alike and ordinary before, were brought to life when someone took the time to make each one unique.

God has taken the time to make each person unique too. The variety He provided makes life interesting. By trying to be just like someone else, I'm ruining God's tremendous act of creativity.

Does not the potter have the right to make out of the same lump of clay some pottery for noble purposes and some for common use? (Rom. 9:21 NIV).

O God, thank You for caring enough to make me a unique individual. Thank You that I don't have to try to be like anyone else. Amen.

December 15

IT IS THE LORD!

Jesus appeared to His disciples several times after He rose from the dead. On one such occasion, He stood on the shore, calling to those who were fishing on the lake. John was the first to recognize Him. He knew that only Jesus could cause their nets to be full of fish.

When Jesus appears today, too often I fail to recognize Him. When I look, I can see Him in birds, people, trees, attitudes, and circumstances. Then He gives me the opportunity to say, "It is the Lord!"

Then the disciple whom Jesus loved said to Peter, "It is the Lord!" (John 21:7 NIV).

Thank You, Lord, for making Yourself real to me in many situations. Grant that I will recognize You more often in the details of each day. Amen.

December 16

HEART TO HEART

December is a busy month as people prepare for the Christmas season. At this time of the year, as at any busy time, I need to make a special effort to spend some time each day with my Lord. It's not always easy to make time, but if I'm sincere, it's always worthwhile.

I am inspired by the words of Henry Drummond: "Five minutes spent in the companionship of Christ every morning, Ay, two minutes, if it is face to face and heart to heart, will change the whole day."

I screamed, "I'm slipping, Lord!" and he was kind and saved me (Ps. 94:18 LB).

Father, forgive me for the times when I should have stopped to talk to You but didn't. Thank You for helping me when I ask for Your guidance and for being patient when I forget. Amen.

December 17

GOD'S PRESENCE

I once heard a story about a visiting preacher, who wondered why the church in which he was preaching smelled so good. Upon asking for their secret, he learned that most of the people of that congregation worked in a perfume factory. The aroma stayed with them and gave fragrance to the entire church building.

If I spend time in God's presence, it will affect those around me, just as the perfume was evident on the factory workers. His distinctive qualities of love and goodness will radiate from me. Only by living in God's presence can I show forth His Spirit.

For in him we live and move and have our being (Acts 17:28 NIV).

I pray, Father, that Your presence in me will be evident to all those around me. May I keep it that way by remaining in Your presence. Amen.

SNOWFLAKES

A snowflake is a beautiful phenomenon. Some people may not like countless snowflakes piled up and in need of being shoveled off the sidewalks, or the coldness they bring, but each separate flake is an interesting work of art. They all look alike until they're observed more closely. Then it becomes clear that each one is different. If God cares enough to send something as beautiful as a snowflake to me, even though I often neglect to enjoy its beauty, how much more must He care for me!

> **O Lord, what a variety you have made! And in wisdom you have made them all! The earth is full of your riches (Ps. 104:24 LB).**

Lord, Your artwork is fantastic! Thank You for the beauty in small everyday things. Amen.

THE GREATEST KING

Jesus came quietly into the world of which He was to become King. Few people were expecting the arrival of the one whose name would be exalted above all names, but that didn't seem to bother anyone. Joseph and Mary calmly accepted a stable for His birth, the shepherds rejoiced, and the wise men chose not to spread the news to Herod.

Many didn't recognize Jesus as the greatest man ever born; in fact many rejected Him; but that didn't make His life worth any less. When I'm tempted to feel rejected and worthless, I can remember how the greatest King who ever lived was also rejected by men.

The stone the builders rejected has become the capstone; the Lord has done this, and it is marvelous in our eyes (Mark 12:10,11 NIV).

Jesus my King, help me to see that to be the greatest doesn't mean that I'll always be accepted. Teach me to do Your will. Amen.

December 20

OBEDIENCE WITH OFFERING

The Christmas season finds people doing many nice things — sending cards of appreciation to friends, giving the newspaper boy an extra tip, singing carols to old folks and the poor, giving gifts and baking for lots of company. All of these are enjoyable as well as good; but I need to ask myself in the midst of it all if what I'm doing is really honoring Jesus.

Examples in the Bible teach that God doesn't always accept the offerings of men. He is not interested in them unless obedience to Him is also given. I must ask myself if in all the Christmas activities I'm trying to impress men or obey God.

Has the Lord as much pleasure in your burnt offerings and sacrifices as in your obedience? Obedience is far better than sacrifice (1 Sam. 15:22 LB).

Dear Jesus, let me not think good acts alone will please You. Guide me in keeping Your will in all that I do. Amen.

December 21

WHAT DID YOU GIVE?

"What did you get for Christmas?"
"Did you get everything you wanted?"
These kinds of questions are not uncommon after

Christmas gifts are opened. I had asked them many times myself until last year when a new thought struck me. A friend and I were wondering why we ask people these questions if we truly believe the verse that says it is more blessed to give than to receive. We decided to ask people what they *gave* for Christmas instead. At first many were caught off guard because it wasn't the normal question and they began to tell what they'd received. But when they finally caught on, their smiles showed that they, too, understood that what is given is the most important.

It is more blessed to give than to receive (Acts 20:35 NIV).

Thank You, Lord, for the resources I have from which I can give to others. Keep me mindful of the importance of giving. Amen.

December 22

BE A GOOD RECEIVER

Even though it is more blessed to give than to receive, it is also a necessary skill to be able to receive graciously. I have always gotten joy out of giving, but until recently I didn't realize the importance of receiving.

A friend and I were eating at a restaurant one evening. To show my appreciation of her friendship, I wanted to pay for her meal but she refused my offer. She insisted that she could afford it better than I could. She didn't realize the joy I would have had in doing it, or the hurt I felt when I was turned down.

From that incident I've learned how crucial it is to be a good receiver. This Christmas especially I want to make my appreciation more evident.

If a man's gift is . . . contributing to the needs of others, let him give generously (Rom. 12:6,8 NIV).

Grant, O God, that I will be a gracious receiver. Teach me the joy of receiving as well as giving. Amen.

December 23

MORE THAN A CELEBRATION

As Christmas draws near and celebrations, pretty decorations, and parties are at their height, it's easy to become caught up in the activities and forget the true meaning of Christmas. The traditional manger scene of the baby Jesus and His birth is beautiful, and everyone loves the story, praising God for sending His Son.

But the enthusiasm is lost after Christmas when we study Jesus' growth and ministry. Adoring the baby Jesus is easier than following Jesus as Lord. Christmas is more than a joyful celebration. It is a plea for a mature commitment to Christ to be His representatives on earth.

And a voice from heaven said, "This is my Son, whom I love, with him I am well-pleased" (Matt. 3:17 NIV).

Son of God, guide me in my love for You, that You will be glorified as Lord, not just adored as a baby. Amen.

December 24

THE BEST THING THAT HAPPENED

When I see a beautiful view, hear a good joke, or experience something new and exciting, my first reaction is to share it with someone. I can't keep all the joy to myself.

Neither could the angels keep their joy suppressed when Jesus was born. Many came from heaven to tell the shepherds of His glory. Jesus' birth and entrance into my life is the greatest thing that has happened to me. If I long to share many smaller things with my friends, how much more should I be sharing with them the good news of Jesus — especially if they don't know it yet.

Christmas is a good time to begin telling those I come in contact with about the best thing that has happened in my life.

Suddenly a great company of the heavenly host appeared with the angel, praising God and saying, "Glory to God in the highest, and on earth peace to men on whom his favor rests" (Luke 2:13,14 NIV).

Thank You, Father, for sending Your Son to the world. I praise His name. Guide me in sharing the good news of His birth and life with those around me. Amen.

December 25

LOVE GIFT

Each year, my sister and I try to surprise mother with a birthday cake. And every year, something goes wrong and the cake is a flop. But mother always acts as if it's the best cake she's ever tasted. She appreciates the love that goes into making it and hardly notices that we messed it up.

On Christmas, when I like to give gifts, I must remember the lesson she has taught me. A gift, no matter how small or inexpensive, is worth much if I give it out of love. Just as God gave His Son in love, I want to give in love.

Above all, love each other deeply, because love covers over a multitude of sins (1 Peter 4:8 NIV).

Thank You, Father, for Your Son — the most loving gift I have ever received. May I give gifts with the same loving attitude. Amen.

CHRISTMAS ISN'T OVER

Christmas Day is past for another year, but is Christmas over?

I like what Dale Evans Rogers says about it: "Christmas, my child, is love in action. . . . When you love someone, you give to them, as God gives to us. The greatest gift He ever gave was the Person of His Son, sent to us in human form so that we might know what God the Father is really like! Every time we love, every time we give, it's Christmas."

So December 25 is really just a take-off point for countless more Christmas experiences throughout the coming year!

> **For unto us a Child is born; unto us a Son is given; and the government shall be upon his shoulder. These will be his royal titles: "Wonderful," "Counselor," "The Mighty God," "The Everlasting Father," "The Prince of Peace" (Isa. 9:6 LB).**

Thank You, Jesus, not only for one, but 365 days of Christmas a year. Amen.

UNEARNED LOVE

When someone does me a favor, I often feel as if I don't deserve it, and I try to think of how to repay the kindness. True love, however, is never earned; it must be given. God's love and forgiveness are difficult for my human mind to conceive of, but they cannot be earned. It is His gift to each one who has enough faith to believe in Him. Doing things for God must be a result of my relationship with Him, not so I will have a relationship with Him.

> **For it is by grace you have been saved, through faith — and this not from yourselves, it is a gift of God (Eph. 2:8 NIV).**

Thank You, Father, for Your gift of love and forgiveness. Grant that I will not try to earn these gifts, but that I will act because of them. Amen.

THE CROSS

A few years ago I received a cross necklace from a friend. It was to remind me of the power I could have from Jesus when I was willing to ask Him to guide my life. The cross became a reminder of Jesus' life of continual giving of Himself.

Christmas and Easter are closely tied together. Jesus came to give His life for the sins of the world. Therefore, to be a follower of His means that I, too, must be willing to give of myself for His purposes.

> **Therefore, I urge you, brothers, in view of God's mercy, to offer yourselves as living sacrifices, holy and pleasing to God — which is your spiritual worship (Rom. 12:1 NIV).**

Dear Jesus, keep me ever mindful of the need to give myself as a sacrifice for Your work. Thank You for the privilege to share in Your mercy. Amen.

December 29

LOVE AT HOME

We sometimes sing the hymn "Love at Home." The first line says, "There is beauty all around when there's love at home."

I sometimes take the love I have at home for granted. Love in the broader sense, in the Christian family, is sometimes taken for granted too. I forget that without love, there could be no real beauty. Jesus was born to bring God's love to the world. Through His love, I can have real joy and beauty.

Therefore love is the fulfillment of the law (Rom. 13:10 NIV).

Thank You, almighty God, for your love that surrounds me with beauty. May I be a useful channel through which to keep love alive. Amen.

December 30

REVOLUTION IN RESOLUTIONS

As one year comes to a close, many people are making resolutions for the year to come. Whether the past year was a good one or marked with many failures, everyone hopes the new year will be better. High hopes are also put on a better life in the Lord. But why are good intentions so often not carried out?

Part of the reason may be that the resolutions don't become revolutions. I resolve that I want God to control my life, but I forget to make Him Lord over everything and make a revolution of my life. In the coming year I don't want to merely make resolutions, but also let God turn them into revolutions.

And I will give you a new heart — I will give you new and right desires — and put a new spirit within you (Ezek. 36:26 LB).

Mold my life, O God, in the coming year. Turn the good intentions of my resolutions into revolutions in my life. Amen.

December 31

INVENTORY

Another year is almost over. It's time to look back over the past year and see what needs to be changed in my life.

More importantly, it's time to look ahead and be ready for all the things God has in store for me in the coming year. Each year has more in it than I'm ready to handle alone, but with Jesus as a constant friend to help me with each step, it will be the best year yet.

> **He has delivered us from such a deadly peril, and he will deliver us. On him we have set our hope that he will continue to deliver us (2 Cor. 1:10 NIV).**

Lord, I commit the coming year to Your work in my life, and I commit my life to You to use in whatever way You desire. Amen.